TEST YOUR
Countercultural
LITERACY

TEST YOUR
Countercultural
LITERACY

Kathy A. Zahler
Diane Zahler

ARCO
New York

First Edition

 ARCO

Simon & Schuster, Inc.
Gulf+Western Building
One Gulf+Western Plaza
New York, NY 10023

DISTRIBUTED BY PRENTICE HALL TRADE SALES

Manufactured in the United States of America

1   2   3   4   5   6   7   8   9   10

Library of Congress Cataloging-in-Publication Data

Zahler, Kathy A.
Test your countercultural literacy / Kathy A. Zahler, Diane
Zahler.
    p.   cm.
  Bibliography: p.
  ISBN 0-13-911983-3
    1. United States—History—1961–1969—Miscellanea.   2. United
States—History—1969– —Miscellanea.   3. United States—Social
conditions—1960–1980—Miscellanea.   4. United States—Popular
culture—History—20th century—Miscellanea.   5. Questions and
answers.   I. Zahler, Diane.   II. Title.
E841.Z34   1989   89-34928
973.92—dc20   CIP

Contents

Acknowledgments

Thanks especially to Mark, whose idea it was, and to Philip, as always.

Our appreciation to GK, JW, and RG for their suggestions and advice. And to Catherine, who was barely alive at the time but still managed to ask the right questions.

Photo Credits

Front Cover

Top left: Janis Joplin: AP / Wide World Photos
Top right: Bob Dylan: AP / Wide World Photos
Bottom left: Allen Ginsberg: © by Fred W. McDarrah

Back Cover

Top center: Timothy Leary: AP / Wide World Photos
Top right: Aretha Franklin: Michael Ochs Archive
Middle right: Abbie Hoffman: © by Fred W. McDarrah
Bottom left: Ravi Shankar: AP / Wide World Photos

Introduction

Writing *Test Your Cultural Literacy* (1988) forced us to confront some Big Questions: Whose culture is it, anyway? Who defines culture? Where is the line that separates lore from trivia, and who determines that separation? At the time, we said that we believe the national stockpile of "required" background knowledge is not static; it changes over time, albeit far more slowly than external events might dictate.

In thinking it over, however, it occurs to us that this implies a gradual, standardized evolution. Indeed, the change *is* sometimes gradual, but sometimes a sudden, drastic correction takes place. With such a sudden shift, an astonishing amount of new information may suddenly be loaded onto the stockpile, displacing or covering up material already there. A radical correction of that kind took place in this country during the 1960s.

In a relatively short period of time, corrections were made or begun in the areas of race, gender, politics, and interpersonal relationships. Old words received new connotations: *black, sister, hawk,* and even *family.* Old stereotypes toppled: the subservient person of color, the happy housewife, the infallible president, the obedient child. Old laws changed, altering old roles. Old methods of politicking and waging war no longer worked. Old rules governing schools, workplaces, and families were challenged and often overturned.

It is strange to talk to today's students: Yes, there really was a time when people took in the homeless, when people risked their lives to be able to vote, when people cared so much about what the government did that they traveled thousands of miles to express their displeasure. Did it really happen? Well, yes—and no. First, we have to accept the fact that when we say "people," we are—and always were—talking about a minority within a large and powerful society. Second, we must recognize the enormous variations in goals and methods of the members of that minority. There was not one movement; there were many.

To study the counterculture in the sixties is to see a variety of groups running one step ahead of mass culture's great levelers: television, *Time* magazine, Hollywood. During the sixties, the media achieved their present dominion over the making and breaking of political figures and social movements. For that reason, this is an excellent era in which to see the narrow line that separates counterculture from culture and observe the process by which subcultures are co-opted and subsumed into the elite idiom, the ruling society.

Definitions

The period known as the sixties is defined differently for different purposes. In this book it will extend from the election of President Kennedy, 1960, to 1973, when the peace settlement in Paris led to the withdrawal of U.S. troops from Vietnam. This is as arbitrary as anyone else's definition, but it allows us, at one end, to discuss early aspects of the civil rights movement and, at the other end, to touch on important issues in the women's movement.

When we talk about culture in this book, we refer to American culture; when we talk about counterculture, we are confining our remarks to a slice of American history. The term *counterculture,* when applied to the sixties, is often used to refer only to the hippies. Theodore Roszak, who popularized the term, made it quite clear that he considered the New Left countercultural as well. Although the hippies and the political activists stemmed from different sources, both were moving toward

> . . . a reorganization of the prevailing state of personal and social consciousness . . . [f]rom a culture that has a longstanding, entrenched commitment to an

egocentric and intellective mode of consciousness
. . . toward a sense of identity that is communal and
nonintellective.[1]

He compares this state of affairs to "the disjuncture between
Greco-Roman rationality and Christian mystery" in the Roman Empire during the first centuries A.D.[2] Whether or not
one accepts his definition and comparison, Roszak imbues
the youth culture of the sixties with the power to influence
a major shift in the consciousness of an entire society.

So we include hippies and student radicals in our look
at the counterculture, but we also include members of certain
discrete cultures within American society: African-Americans, Native Americans, and others whose cultures either
influenced the counterculture or became a part of the movement to correct existing definitions of culture.

Why Study the Sixties?

Was there ever a more overanalyzed decade, or one more
disputed? A common bit of folklore recently bruited about
by conservative revisionists is that the sixties were less a
correction than an aberration; that the real correction came
in the seventies when the country slid back into a comfortable
conservatism. It is easy to pretend that nothing happened.
Eighteen-year-olds can vote—but many still do not. Women
hold executive positions—but most are still paid less than
men. Civil rights legislation is on the books—but according
to census figures, the percentage of African-Americans living
in poverty is three times that of whites. What is the real
legacy of the sixties?

When the decade began, the baby boomers, children born
after World War II, were just becoming a force in the market.

1. Theodore Roszak, "Youth and the Great Refusal," *The Nation*
   206 (March 25, 1968), 404.

2. Ibid.

In 1960 there were 24 million Americans between the ages of 15 and 24; by 1970 there were 35 million.[3] These children were better educated than any previous generation; college enrollment doubled over the course of the decade.[4] For the first time the youth of America were a power to be reckoned with and to be pandered to—by the media, the music business, and producers of consumer goods. By 1960 over 87 percent of American households had television; by 1970 the figure was close to 95 percent.[5] These statistics seem unrelated, but the realities they represent came together in the sixties and changed forever the way our culture evolves.

Television does not reflect; it magnifies. It is the nature of the medium to magnify everything to the same power, thus glorifying some issues while trivializing others. In addition, like the rest of the media, television is selective and restrictive. "One issue at a time gets singled out . . . and then gets shuttled out of sight, often falsely implying that the problem has been resolved."[6] How are issues selected? What makes an issue newsworthy? The market for commercial programming comes into play here. When youth is the market, the interests of youth are newsworthy.

The interests of youth are often at odds with the interests usually reflected by corporate media, the interests of the power elite. What political philosopher Antonio Gramsci calls *ideological hegemony*, control by the ruling class through imposition of its definitions on the world,[7] came into conflict

3. Herb Hendler, *Year by Year in the Rock Era* (New York: Praeger, 1987), 134.

4. Ibid., 104.

5. Austin Ranney, *Channels of Power: The Impact of Television on American Politics* (New York: Basic Books, 1983), 8.

6. Donald Lazere, "Introduction: Entertainment as Social Control," in *American Media and Mass Culture: Left Perspectives* (Berkeley: University of California Press, 1987), 11.

7. Antonio Gramsci, *Prison Notebooks: Selections*, trans. Quintin Hoare and Geoffrey N. Smith (New York: International Publishing, 1971). Todd Gitlin applies the concept of hegemony to mass media in "Television's Screens: Hegemony in Transition" in

at times in the sixties with the dollar power of the youth market. The result was an uneasy give-and-take, with the media tentatively covering issues such as SDS and antiwar activists because of their appeal to youth but assigning their own definitions to movements and individuals so that corporate interests were not threatened or overshadowed.[8] Radicals became "peaceniks"; hippies were renamed "the Love Generation" or "the flower children"; even acid rock was watered down to "psychedelic rock," and its once-reviled sounds were moderated, neutered, and used in commercial jingles. We name our world in order to control and own it; the media do the same thing.

Newspapers had always defined and classified politicians—the *Los Angeles Times* invented and fostered Richard Nixon, for example.[9] Television and the powerful news magazines sped up the process and made it visual. They brought the gory parts of war into the living room; they anointed the good-looking, manageable spokespeople; they made fashion out of ideas. They ensured that the person or group that best managed the media controlled the defining process. Without the ascension of the media in the sixties, we could never have had eight years of President Reagan in the eighties, nor could we now have a national news program

American Media and Mass Culture: Left Perspectives (Berkeley: University of California Press, 1987) and in *The Whole World Is Watching: Mass Media in the Making and Unmaking of the New Left* (Berkeley: University of California Press, 1980). For an application of a similar framework, which the authors call a "propaganda model," to coverage of the war in Vietnam, Laos, and Cambodia, see Edward S. Herman and Noam Chomsky, *Manufacturing Consent: The Political Economy of the Mass Media* (New York: Pantheon, 1988), 169–296.

8. Todd Gitlin shows the effect of this on SDS in *The Whole World Is Watching* (Berkeley: University of California Press, 1980).

9. For a detailed look at how this occurred and a great overall picture of the rise of the media, see David Halberstam, *The Powers That Be* (New York: Alfred A. Knopf, 1979). To see how Nixon learned to use visual media to his advantage, see Joe McGinniss, *The Selling of the President* (New York: Pocket Books, 1968).

(ABC) that refers to itself, apparently without irony, as "the program that sets the American agenda." Not "reflects," "sets."

Before the sixties, much of American culture was defined locally—in communities, schools, churches, hometown newspapers. The sixties saw the rise to power of the mass media and a new process of naming the world, one that is less parochial but by its very global nature is also less precise, less heterodox, and ultimately less meaningful for the audience that receives the prepackaged definitions. To study the sixties, then, is to study a time of great change in the way we look at the world, a time during which the slow, steady process of defining our culture accelerated, and we, the people, lost control.

The Tests

There are ten tests of forty questions each. We begin with a test called "Roots of the Counterculture," rejecting the idea that the sixties sprang full-formed from the void. Here we look at ideas and trends that made the era possible. The next test sets the stage; it is called "Background Issues and Events." This deals with events around the world that shaped the era: the Vietnam War, decolonialization in Africa, the Great Society. The remaining tests focus on the counterculture: "Politics and Protest," "Civil Rights and Liberation," "Geography," "Art, Performance, and Media," "Music," "Lifestyles," "Quotes, Phrases, and Symbols," and "Literature."

The items are multiple-choice, and four possibilities are listed for each:

18. Mescaline is the active substance in a drug produced from

   a. poppies

   b. mushrooms

   c. mandrake

   d. cacti

In many cases, either you will know the answer or you won't. In other cases, you may be able to come up with the correct answer through a process of elimination.

How Did You Do?

When you complete a test, use the explanatory answers that follow the test to check your responses. The answers will help you determine *why* your response was correct or incorrect and may increase your knowledge of the subject.

18. **(d)** Kiowa and Navaho Indians used the peyote cactus in religious ceremonies long before the powers of the plant were discovered by other Americans. The Aztec people had used peyote for centuries. The active substance that gives the cactus its hallucinatory power is called mescaline. The dried tops of the cactus are called peyote buttons, and it is this form of the plant that is most often used in rituals. In the 1950s, mescaline became available in crystal form, usually powdered and inserted into capsules. Aldous Huxley popularized the drug with his 1954 essay *The Doors of Perception*.

Use the Scoring Key that follows this Introduction to grade yourself.

What Should You Do Now?

Where you were in the sixties will determine your score on these tests. If you were six years old at the time, the questions may seem trivial to you, but one person's trivia is another person's cultural literacy. It will be interesting to see which questions you consider cultural rather than countercultural. If you study Andy Warhol and Nikki Giovanni in college, does that remove them from the latter category and place them in the former? How much of what we considered countercultural in the sixties was absorbed into the culture? To what extent did it have to be diluted or renamed in order for that to happen?

What you do about your gaps in knowledge is up to you. You can begin with our suggestions in the Bibliography. These are works that we found helpful, but they are only the tip of the iceberg when it comes to examining this much-analyzed era. They in turn will lead you to other works, and so on.

We think it is important to understand that the era we cover in this book was not an aberration but rather was a logical part of a process. The war in Vietnam followed logically from the United States's pattern of cold war intercession and hegemonic activity, a pattern that continues today.[10] Antiwar activism arose from movements that already existed, made headlines when it became clear that the war was unprofitable and activism was salable, and diversified in the seventies into the ecology movement and antinuclear activism. Women's liberation, in hibernation from the early part

10. For a view of recent hegemonic processes as carried out by mass media, see Edward W. Said, *Covering Islam* (New York: Pantheon, 1981).

of the century, woke up in the late 1960s and went on to seat women in boardrooms, courtrooms, and smoke-filled rooms over the next two decades. Civil rights gathered strength from churches and union movements, and although the headlines have dwindled, the fight goes on. Understanding the sixties helps us understand where we are now; recognizing the role of the era in the continuum of American and world history allows us to put it in perspective and to realize that it is not just the past but is part of the future as well. As the abolitionist Wendell Phillips once said, "Revolutions are not made; they come. A revolution is as natural a growth as an oak. It comes out of the past. Its foundations are laid far back."

True literacy enables us to make informed decisions and to construct our own philosophy of the world. To reach this goal, we must understand our past and how it informs our present, and we must recognize the ways in which our view of the world is shaped by external forces. To understand ourselves and our place in the world, to see the "big picture," we may sometimes need to break the bonds of culture and rise above it—a lesson from the counterculture that we ignore at our peril.

KAZahler

February 17, 1989

SCORING KEY

Score one point for each correct answer.

35—40	*Excellent.* You probably still have love beads and a Stop the War button somewhere in the back of the closet—dust them off and wear them with pride.
30—34	*Good.* You secretly watch "thirtysomething" and "The Cosby Show" but pretend they aren't about you. Control your yuppie tendencies and return to your roots.
25—29	*Fair.* Did you whine because coverage of the 1968 Convention ate into reruns of "I Love Lucy"? Were you really paying attention?
20—24	*Poor.* Unless you were born after 1970, you clearly deserve to have an ex-CIA chief as your president.
Below 20	*Time for literacy training.* See the Bibliography in the back of this book.

On the Road: Roots of the Counterculture

The people, and the people alone, are the motive force in the making of world history.

—MAO ZEDONG

1. Which of the following works are by the 1950s beat author Jack Kerouac?
   a. *Empty Mirror* and *Kaddish and Other Poems*
   b. *On the Road* and *The Dharma Bums*
   c. *One Flew Over the Cuckoo's Nest* and *Sometimes a Great Notion*
   d. *Naked Lunch* and *Junk*

2. Who was Jacques Ellul?
   a. a French Marxist who wrote in the 1950s about revolution and Christian social activism
   b. a French socialist who led political campaigns against France's colonial war in Vietnam in the 1950s
   c. a 1950s French painter whose works paved the way for the art movements of the 1960s
   d. a French priest who preached against France's use of torture against Algerian rebels

3. Why was rock and roll important in the culture of the 1950s?
   a. It led directly to increased popularity for social-protest folk music.
   b. It sparked feelings of freedom and anticonformist rebelliousness among young people.
   c. Its rural origins awakened Americans to the problems of the rural poor.
   d. Its lyrics helped make the public aware of America's role in the Korean War.

4. Who was the "Organization Man" described in a popular 1950s book?
   a. the ambitious man who seeks power through a career in important governmental organizations
   b. the social rebel who joins the ranks of organized crime

c. the middle-class man who lives by the values of corporate big business

d. the political rebel who organizes mass movements to seize governmental power

5. What did the French author Simone de Beauvoir do in 1949 to prepare the way for the 1960s?

   a. She wrote the best-selling novel *Bonjour Tristesse.*

   b. She wrote *The Second Sex,* a classic of feminist literature.

   c. She became the most radical of France's "New Wave" film directors.

   d. She wrote the existentialist classic *Being and Nothingness.*

6. What was the aim of the 1950s British protest movement known as CND?

   a. to rid the world of nuclear weapons

   b. to press for independence for Britain's African colonies

   c. to fight for equality for Britain's growing nonwhite immigrant population

   d. to prevent British participation in the war in Korea

7. Who was the "white Negro" described in a widely read 1958 essay?

   a. the white man or woman who marched in support of civil rights for blacks

   b. the poor white in the South

   c. the black who sought entry into the white power structure

   d. the white hipster who absorbed the alienation felt by blacks

8. What major lesson did young leftists around the world draw from the Chinese Revolution of 1949?

  a. Peaceful marches and demonstrations can lead to revolution.

  b. Chinese culture is naturally suited to a Communist system.

  c. A Communist revolution can be made by other social classes besides urban workers.

  d. A country that has a revolution is likely to attack its neighbors.

9. What landmark event took place in Little Rock, Arkansas, in 1957?

  a. Federal troops were sent in to enforce a school desegregation order.

  b. A Northern civil rights worker was lynched by Ku Klux Klansmen.

  c. A rock-and-roll single was played on the radio for the first time.

  d. Students from throughout the country gathered to plan a campaign of leftist organizing.

10. What percentage of American homes had television as the 1960s began?

  a. 55%

  b. 75%

  c. 90%

  d. 40%

11. What famous beat poem of 1956 begins, "I saw the best minds of my generation destroyed by madness . . ."?

  a. "Kaddish"

  b. "Howl"

c. "Landscapes of Living and Dying"

d. "Star"

12. What did a woman named Rosa Parks do in 1955 to help launch the modern black civil rights movement?

a. She became the first black woman to be elected to Congress.

b. She wrote a stirring manifesto on black women's rights.

c. She became the first black to be crowned Miss America.

d. She refused to move to the back of a segregated bus.

13. Margaret Sanger helped pave the way for the 1960s counterculture through her pioneering work in

a. the study of women's sexuality, a major issue for the growing feminist movement

b. the development of LSD and other hallucinogenic drugs

c. the promotion of birth control, which made the sexual revolution possible

d. the reporting of sympathetic news accounts from inside mainland China

14. The term "red diaper baby" was used in the 1950s to describe

a. babies whose parents followed the instructions of Dr. Spock

b. the children of members of America's Old Left

c. the first generation of Chinese born after the 1949 revolution

d. children who had been exposed to radiation from atom bomb tests

15. Which of the following organizations was the main forerunner of Students for a Democratic Society (SDS)?

  a. the National Student Association

  b. the League for Industrial Democracy

  c. the Young People's Socialist League

  d. the Non-Violent Action Group

16. What did the Surrealist artists of the 1920s and 1930s bequeath to the 1960s counterculture?

  a. a fascination with the human unconscious as revealed in dreams

  b. painting techniques in which broken color is used to depict visual images

  c. the concept of revolution against naturalism to achieve a spiritual reality

  d. the concepts of individualism and self-reliance

17. What was the result of the 1955 U.S. Supreme Court case *Brown v. Board of Education?*

  a. Segregation in public schools was outlawed.

  b. Abortion for school-age girls was legalized.

  c. Segregation in public schools in the South was upheld.

  d. Freedom of the press as it applies to school newspapers was upheld.

18. How did Jean-Paul Sartre, Sören Kierkegaard, and Martin Heidegger contribute to the intellectual culture of the 1960s?

  a. by writing beat poetry and fiction

  b. by advocating mysticism and the study of Eastern religions

  c. by developing the philosophy called existentialism

  d. by calling for a return to an earlier tradition of logical positivism

19. Who was the "quiet American" in a prophetic 1955 novel by Graham Greene?

   a. a power-hungry general who threatens to start a nuclear war

   b. a Socialist politician who seeks greater cooperation with the Soviet Union

   c. an innocent soldier who is sent into combat in Korea

   d. a naive idealist whose misguided efforts lead to conflict in Vietnam

20. The pioneering American Socialist Eugene V. Debs was an inspiration to early 1960s activists because of his

   a. belief in nonviolent social change

   b. belief that workers' unions were useless

   c. belief that America needed a third major political party

   d. belief that communism was the best political system

21. What goal did the organization called CORE pursue in the 1940s and 1950s?

   a. an end to racial discrimination through nonviolent action

   b. equal employment opportunity for women

   c. truth in advertising and consumer aid

   d. establishment of a separate black state

22. The psychologist Wilhelm Reich became known in the 1950s for his controversial studies of

   a. the sex instinct and life energy

   b. hallucinogenic drug use in Native American cultures

   c. aggressive behavior in mammals

   d. the effects of poverty on personality development

23. Woody Guthrie, who first gained fame in the 1930s, was a great influence on such 1960s figures as

   a. Ultra Violet and Edie Sedgewick

    b. Joan Baez and Bob Dylan

    c. Malcolm X and Huey Newton

    d. Abbie Hoffman and Jerry Rubin

24. Ernesto Guevara, an Argentine, was idolized by many 1960s militants as

    a. a poet and preacher of pacifism

    b. a painter of left-wing political murals

    c. a philosopher and critic of the oppressive features of Western society

    d. a guerrilla fighter and revolutionary activist

25. What did the Indian leader Mohandas K. Gandhi bequeath to the 1960s counterculture?

    a. the concept of redistribution of resources within the community

    b. the use of nonviolent civil disobedience as a means of achieving reforms

    c. the concept of corporate liberalism

    d. all of the above

26. The leftist group that was the main rival of the fledgling SDS was

    a. the Young People's Socialist League

    b. the Young Communist League

    c. the Marxist-Leninist Youth party

    d. the Young Americans for Socialism

27. In the 1955 film *Rebel Without a Cause,* James Dean provided a role model for

    a. activists seeking to overthrow a government they viewed as corrupt

    b. youths alienated from the values of their parents' generation

    c. future members of the silent majority

    d. pacifists committed to a life of nonviolence

28. The scientist Rachel Carson helped launch one part of the 1960s counterculture with a book that

 a. predicted increasing psychological alienation in the nuclear age

 b. challenged Freudian dogma about women's subconscious

 c. warned of the increasing pollution of the natural environment

 d. revealed government plans to build a neutron bomb

29. What landmark event occurred in Cuba on New Year's Day, 1959?

 a. Guerrillas led by Fidel Castro overthrew the regime of Fulgencio Batista y Zaldívar.

 b. The Soviet Union, under pressure from a U.S. blockade, agreed to withdraw missiles it had placed there.

 c. Fidel Castro's rebel forces staged an unsuccessful attack against the army barracks at Santiago.

 d. With CIA support, anti-Castro Cuban exiles attempted an armed invasion.

30. The organization known as SANE, founded in 1957, originally sought to

 a. promote America's space program following the Soviets' launch of *Sputnik*

 b. challenge America's traditional two-party system

 c. ban use of the atomic bomb

 d. protest racial segregation in public facilities in the South

31. The pioneering black social activist A. Philip Randolph was the founder of

 a. the National Student Association

 b. the Brotherhood of Sleeping Car Porters

   c. the Spartacist League

   d. the Southern Christian Leadership Conference

32. The young Socialist activist Michael Harrington stirred public concern in 1959 with his widely read article on

   a. the Army–McCarthy hearings

   b. the possibilities for nuclear disarmament

   c. the benefits of urban renewal

   d. the continuing widespread existence of poverty in America

33. Norman Thomas, America's best-known Socialist from the 1920s through the 1950s,

   a. ran for president six times

   b. advocated the abolition of organized religion

   c. was imprisoned for supporting the Chinese revolution

   d. blindly followed the dictates of the Soviet Union

34. In a 1955 novel that came to symbolize an era, Sloan Wilson wrote about a

   a. black man trying to find himself in urban Chicago

   b. middle-aged suburbanite increasingly alienated from the world

   c. high school student rebelling against authority

   d. young housewife on the verge of a nervous breakdown

35. A 1956 book that criticized the decision makers in American society was

   a. *The Power Elite* by C. Wright Mills

   b. *The Structure of Social Action* by Talcott Parsons

   c. *The End of Ideology* by Daniel Bell

   d. *The Age of Reform* by Richard Hofstadter

36. The 1950s group known as the "Angry Young Men" were

   a. the leaders of the student organization that later became SDS

   b. a circle of class-conscious young English playwrights and novelists

   c. an organization of militants dedicated to stopping the Korean War

   d. a circle of Abstract Expressionist painters in New York

37. The eminent British author Aldous Huxley was admired in the 1960s counterculture for his

   a. ideologically committed plays and poetry celebrating the class struggle

   b. exhaustive sociological studies of the urban poor

   c. superbly crafted screenplays for early television drama programs

   d. descriptions of his experiments with hallucinogens

38. In 1957, the Reverend Martin Luther King, Jr., became the head of the civil rights organization called the

   a. Alabama Christian Movement for Human Rights

   b. Freedom Democratic party

   c. Southern Christian Leadership Conference

   d. National Association for the Advancement of Colored People

39. The Port Huron Statement, the founding manifesto of SDS written in 1962 by Tom Hayden, proposed that students take over the reforming role once played by

   a. the Minutemen

   b. the government

   c. the Socialist party

   d. organized labor

40. The pioneering educator John Dewey influenced 1960s reformers with his belief that

   a. education should concentrate on the study of beauty

   b. the individual must be at the center of any educational experience

   c. science should be the center of any school curriculum

   d. all study is a search for nirvana or enlightenment

TEST 1: Explanatory Answers

1. **(b)** Jack Kerouac was one of the foremost beat writers, a name he took from the word *beatific*. He and authors Allen Ginsberg, Lawrence Ferlinghetti, Gregory Corso, and William S. Burroughs formed a literary movement that rejected middle-class values and focused instead on rebellious individualism, pacifism, and enhancement of consciousness through jazz, sexual experience, and drugs. This philosophy strongly influenced the movements of the 1960s. Kerouac's book *On the Road* (1957) is the story of a hitchhiking trip across America and is considered a classic of the beat movement. The other works listed are by Allen Ginsberg, Ken Kesey, and William S. Burroughs.

2. **(a)** Jacques Ellul was a Christian Marxist whose writings criticized modern society, spoke of a new Christian theology, and stressed university reform. A professor of Roman law, he was one of the first advocates of a new forum-style university that would allow students to question and criticize the curriculum. His challenges to social activists, political leftists, and Christians influenced the philosophy of the New Left.

3. **(b)** Rock and roll, a term coined by a Cleveland disc jockey, was a blend of rhythm-and-blues and country-and-western music that was made popular in the 1950s by musicians such as Jerry Lee Lewis, Buddy Holly, and Elvis Presley. Rock and roll was aimed at young people, who were beginning to be recognized as a social force, and its beat and lyrics encouraged feelings of freedom and energy. In the 1960s, rock and roll evolved into rock music, which also incorporated elements of folk music and often addressed social problems and advocated social and political change.

4. **(c)** In *The Organization Man* (1956), William Whyte described the widely noted 1950s sociological phenomenon in which the individualistic values of the traditional Protestant Work Ethic were rapidly giving way to the newer conformist values of the corporate business culture. A house in the suburbs, group social activities, and a middle-class education summed up the life-style of the new Organization Man. Whyte's book challenged the Organization Man to resist the organization, claiming that it led to a deadening of the mind and spirit.

5. **(b)** Simone de Beauvoir (1908–1986) was the lover and intellectual companion of Jean-Paul Sartre. She shared Sartre's existentialist philosophy, expressing it in numerous novels and essays. *The Second Sex* (1953) analyzed the status of women in society and helped lay the groundwork for the women's movement of the 1960s.

6. **(a)** The Campaign for Nuclear Disarmament (CND) was a British peace organization formed in the 1950s. It attracted not just members of leftist groups but also large numbers of young people, and it sponsored mass marches and sit-downs in the streets of London to protest the stockpiling and testing of nuclear weapons. The CND eventually forced the Labour party to endorse unilateral nuclear disarmament (an endorsement that was later reversed). It set a powerful example for similar movements in the United States.

7. **(d)** Norman Mailer's "The White Negro" (1958) was both a definition of post-beat hip society and a call for radical social change. Mailer defined "white Negros" as those hipsters who had taken on black culture and black alienation, and he asserted that if the Negro emerged as a force in American life, such hipsters would pose a major threat to the power of the white Establishment.

8. **(c)** Western leftists of the 1930s and 1940s were committed to the classical theories of Marx, Engels, and Lenin, which saw the urban workers of the developed countries—or a political party representing their interests—as the only group capable of leading a Socialist revolution. The Chinese Revolution of 1949, however, demonstrated that third-world peasants, organized in a guerrilla army, were equally capable of playing this historic role. To many young leftists, the conclusion was obvious: socialism would be won not by the increasingly comfortable workers of Europe and America, but by other groups—third-world guerrillas, oppressed minorities, even students. This belief was a core tenet of 1960s Maoism.

9. **(a)** In 1957 in Little Rock, nine black students sought admittance to the public schools under a federal court desegregation order. Governor Orval Faubus and other local law enforcement officers, backed by crowds of angry whites, refused to allow the students to enter the school building. Eventually President

Eisenhower was forced to send in U.S. troops to protect the students and enforce the court order.

10. **(c)** It was in the 1950s that television entered into most American households, and it was in the 1960s that the medium first gained its dominant position in American culture. Although popular TV shows of the decade ranged from "Car 54, Where Are You?" to "The Patty Duke Show," it was television news that soon brought the Vietnam War into living rooms on a daily basis—and awakened Americans to the horror of the war and the power of the protests against it. As early as 1964, 58 percent of people surveyed by the Roper organization were getting their news from television alone.

11. **(b)** *Howl and Other Poems* by Allen Ginsberg was published in 1956 by the San Francisco bookstore owner Lawrence Ferlinghetti, who was immediately charged with printing obscenity. Charges were eventually dismissed, but the book had already become famous. The poem, addressed to an inmate of a mental hospital, reflects the brutality of modern America and provides an ironic look at contemporary society. "Kaddish" is also by Ginsberg; the other two works are by Lawrence Ferlinghetti and Michael McClure.

12. **(d)** Rosa Parks was a black seamstress who lived in Montgomery, Alabama, where the local segregation law forced blacks to sit in the backs of buses. On December 1, 1955, she refused a bus driver's command to move to the back and give up her seat to a white man, and she was arrested. Martin Luther King, Jr., took on her cause and organized a bus boycott by Montgomery blacks. The boycott leaders were arrested in February, but the protest continued until November 1956, when the Supreme Court outlawed bus segregation.

13. **(c)** Margaret Sanger (1883–1966) was a nurse who promoted birth control as an answer to poverty. She was indicted in 1915 for sending birth control materials through the mail and arrested a year later for opening a birth control clinic in Brooklyn. Public approval for her efforts was overwhelming, however, and she lobbied for birth control laws and established other clinics, gradually winning support from the courts. With the advent of the birth control pill, freeing women from unwanted pregnancies, the sexual revolution began, and free

love—sex without fear of consequences—became a part of the counterculture.

14. **(b)** "Red diaper baby" was a slang term for children whose parents had been leftists in the 1930s and 1940s. Growing up in the 1950s, they often felt particularly alienated—their earliest memories sometimes were of accompanying their parents to demonstrations for the Rosenbergs. Many later joined the New Left, sometimes adopting its most radical stances in defiance of their parents' more traditional beliefs.

15. **(b)** The League for Industrial Democracy (LID) was founded in 1905 as the Intercollegiate Socialist Society. Its aim was to introduce college students to socialism; Jack London, Norman Thomas, and John Reed were early members. Divisions between Socialists and Communists led to continual strife within the organization and its campus wing, the Student League for Industrial Democracy (SLID). By 1960 SLID's philosophy of democratic, pragmatic socialism was attracting student radicals who were wary of the more sectarian Marxist groups, and that year the organization was renamed Students for a Democratic Society (SDS).

16. **(a)** Surrealism was a movement in art and literature that flourished in the 1920s and 1930s. Influenced by Freudian psychoanalytic theory, it attempted to portray the workings of the unconscious mind through the interpretation of dreams. Some important figures in surrealism were André Breton in literature, Jean Cocteau in film, and Salvador Dali and Joan Miró in art. Many of the images and ideas of surrealism found their way into the artistic movements of the 1960s.

17. **(a)** In the 1950s, the Brown family of Topeka, Kansas, sued the school system for forcing their children to go to segregated schools. Eventually, the case was reviewed by the Supreme Court, which in 1955 ruled segregation unconstitutional. The Court stated that integration should take place "with all deliberate speed," a vague wording that many Southern schools chose to stretch to its limits.

18. **(c)** Existentialism, a philosophy first developed in postwar France, begins with the idea that there is no fixed human nature; therefore, people are both free and completely responsible for what they become. For most existentialists, this

condition led to mental anguish; for such thinkers of the 1960s as John Barth and Thomas Pynchon, it gave humankind freedom to make its own choices and develop in a new way. One existentialist work important to the 1960s was Albert Camus's "Rebel" (1951), an essay on the difference between philosophical and political rebellion.

19. **(d)** *The Quiet American* (1955) is a novel about an idealistic American in Saigon who, in a state of blind naiveté, channels American money to a Vietnamese "third force" in an attempt to defeat the Viet Minh. As a result, a bloody conflict involving the United States ensues. *The Quiet American* was made into a film in 1958, but the title character was portrayed as a hero rather than a misguided fool.

20. **(a)** Eugene V. Debs (1855–1926) was a Socialist and union organizer who ran for president five times (in 1900, 1904, 1908, 1912, and 1920) on the Socialist party ticket. He was a pacifist who believed strongly in unionization, and he was imprisoned several times for acting on his beliefs.

21. **(a)** Founded by James Farmer in 1942, the Congress of Racial Equality held its first sit-in that same year. Farmer had previously worked for the Quaker Fellowship of Reconciliation, and his goal was to apply Quaker nonviolent principles to action for desegregation in the South. In 1947, CORE and the Fellowship sponsored the "Journey of Reconciliation," a forerunner of the Freedom Rides. The journey was unsuccessful; many of the riders were arrested and jailed. CORE went on to play a major role in the Freedom Rides of the 1960s. In the mid-1960s CORE rejected the notion of nonviolence and began advocating black separatism.

22. **(a)** Wilhelm Reich (1897–1957) was an Austrian psychologist who attempted to synthesize the works of Marx and Freud. He studied the sex instinct, concluding that blocked sexual impulses lead to anxiety, neurosis, and character disorder. His important work in therapy and research, recorded in *The Sexual Revolution* and *Character Analysis,* was partly discredited by his later search for a biological equivalent to psychic energy that he called *orgone.* He moved to the United States in 1939 and in 1954 was indicted for failing to answer an injunction by the FDA having to do with his orgone therapy. He died in prison.

23. (b) Woodrow Wilson Guthrie (1912–1967) was a folk singer and composer of hundreds of songs, many of them political. His anthems for working people, many composed in the 1930s, were sung throughout the folk era of the 1950s and early 1960s. Guthrie's mix of politics and music directly affected many musicians in the counterculture, and his influence continues to be felt today. Among his best-known compositions are "This Land Is Your Land," "Hard Traveling," and "Union Maid."

24. (d) Disgust with the 1954 CIA-supported overthrow of the progressive regime in Guatemala led Ernesto "Che" Guevara (1928–1967) to advocate worldwide revolution. He lent his support to Fidel Castro during the Cuban Revolution and went on to organize guerrilla fighters in the Congo and in Bolivia before being captured and executed by the Bolivian army in October 1967. His writings and mythos made him a hero to many in North America, and as protest in the United States became more militant, the legend of Che was frequently invoked.

25. (b) The civil disobedience used by Gandhi (1869–1948) to challenge British rule in India became the model for peaceful protest throughout the world, directly influencing the beliefs of Martin Luther King, Jr.

26. (a) The Young People's Socialist League (YPSL), the Socialist party's youth group, was SDS's main rival for adherents in the early 1960s. Many YPSL members, Michael Harrington among them, subscribed to Max Schachtman's idea that the future lay in penetrating the Democratic party and turning it leftward; most were also fiercely anti-Communist. An early effort by YPSL to impose its doctrinaire views on the nonideological SDS was defeated in 1961.

27. (b) *Rebel Without a Cause* (1955), directed by Nicholas Ray, struck a chord with American youth with its realistic portrait of three lost friends. James Dean, Sal Mineo, and Natalie Wood played teenagers alienated from their peers and their parents, searching for a new definition of family and a new set of values.

28. (c) Rachel Carson (1907–1964) was a marine biologist who influenced the ecological movement of the 1960s and 1970s with *Silent Spring* (1962). Her earlier works, *The Sea Around*

Us (1951) and *The Edge of the Sea* (1955), are credited with using elegant prose to educate lay readers about the interaction of people and nature.

29. **(a)** Batista (1901–1973) had dominated Cuban politics since 1933 when he helped to overthrow Gerardo Machado, and he became the country's dictator in 1952. Castro attempted an overthrow in 1953, was imprisoned for two years, and then retired to Mexico to organize a guerrilla army under the name "26th of July Movement." A small force landed in Cuba in 1956, and some of the fighters succeeded in evading government troops and set up a base in the mountains. Continual guerrilla action and the loss of support from the United States led to the downfall of the Batista regime, and Castro assumed power on January 1, 1959.

30. **(c)** The Committee for a Sane Nuclear Policy (SANE) was originally established as an umbrella group for ban-the-bomb protestors in the United States. The Committee was formed by a group of atomic scientists and advocates of world government. By the mid-1960s, members often found themselves at odds with other antiwar activists because of SANE's commitment to peaceful legal action and its anti-Communist stance.

31. **(b)** Asa Philip Randolph (1889–1979) founded an all-black union of railroad workers in 1925 and headed the union until 1968. During World War II, he worked to end job discrimination in the defense industry. He was elected vice-president of the AFL-CIO when the two federations merged in 1955, and at the age of seventy-four he was instrumental in organizing the 1963 March on Washington.

32. **(d)** Michael Harrington's work in the 1950s with Dorothy Day and the Catholic Workers mission on the Bowery in New York led him to write an article about poverty in America that he would later expand into an enormously influential book, *The Other America* (1962). Harrington was a Socialist, a member of the League for Industrial Democracy, and an organizer of the Young People's Socialist League. His speeches and writings made him a hero to the student movement of the early 1960s, but his rigid anticommunism led to a falling out between SDS members and Harrington after the Port Huron convention.

33. **(a)** Norman Thomas (1884–1968) was a Presbyterian minister who went on to lead the Socialist party and was its candidate

for president in 1928, 1932, 1936, 1940, 1944, and 1948. His speeches, antiwar stance, and active recruitment in colleges influenced the student movement in the early 1960s.

34. **(b)** *The Man in the Gray Flannel Suit* became a metaphor for an entire class of commuting businessmen. The protagonist has what seemed to constitute "the good life" in the postwar era, but he feels out of control in a world that is changing far too fast for him.

35. **(a)** C. Wright Mills (1916–1962) was a sociologist at Columbia University. He insisted that social science demanded activism, and this idea was to resonate with many students who heard him speak or who read his books. A trio of his works on social change and the new class system in America were widely read by students in the 1960s: *The New Men of Power: America's Labor Leaders* (1948); *White Collar* (1951); and *The Power Elite* (1956).

36. **(b)** The term comes from the autobiography of philosopher and writer Leslie Allen Paul, *Angry Young Man* (1951). It was applied to a number of writers in England who expressed bitter resentment at the Establishment and its hypocrisy. Perhaps the best example of the attitude is found in John Osborne's play *Look Back in Anger* (1957). A college-educated working-class protagonist finds his ambitions thwarted by the class system and takes out his frustrations on his middle-class wife. Kingsley Amis and Alan Sillitoe were two other writers considered part of this group.

37. **(d)** Aldous Huxley (1894–1963) turned from an interest in social issues to a preoccupation with the life of the mind, and his writings clearly evince that change in his focus. His influence on the counterculture stems from his early experiments with mescaline, which he documented in *The Doors of Perception* (1954) and *Heaven and Hell* (1956). Huxley lectured widely on the visionary experience and the use of psychedelics, but he felt that such enlightenment as the drugs provided should be reserved for an intellectual elite.

38. **(c)** The SCLC was founded in 1957 as a result of the Montgomery bus boycott. It arose from the group of Southern churches that had supported the boycott, and it was designed to continue the nonviolent civil rights work that had gone on in Montgomery. After King's assassination in 1968, Ralph Abernathy took over leadership of the organization.

39. **(d)** Clearly, organized labor had a profound influence on the student movement of the 1960s, whether through supporting organizations with money and people power, or by modeling the tools of dissent: strikes, slowdowns, marches, and rallies. The Port Huron Statement makes the point, however, that the postwar era saw a decline in traditional blue-collar union jobs. This led to a decline in labor's ability to manufacture social change. In addition, Hayden saw a crisis in "vision and program" in the labor movement of the late 1950s and early 1960s.

40. **(b)** John Dewey (1859–1952) was a philosopher and educational reformer who affected the political and educational world of the 1960s in many ways. His form of pragmatism was based on the notion that truth is not absolute; it is used by humans to solve problems, and it must change as those problems change. He applied this theory to education by arguing that schools must reflect the society around them, and the individual child must be at the center of any instructional experience. Perhaps his most famous work is *Democracy and Education* (1916), in which he described the role of education as a tool in maintaining the democratic ideal.

TEST 2

The Times They Are A-Changin': Background Issues and Events

Keep asking me, no matter how long—
On the war in Vietnam, I sing this song—
I ain't got no quarrel with the Viet Cong.

—MUHAMMAD ALI

1. Who exactly were the Viet Cong?
   a. the army of South Vietnam
   b. North Vietnamese soldiers who had infiltrated into South Vietnam
   c. foreign Communists who were attacking the South Vietnamese people
   d. Communist insurgents fighting the government of South Vietnam

2. In addition to massive student and worker strikes, what other important event took place in May 1968 in Paris?
   a. the French government's decision to free all remaining French colonies
   b. the opening of peace talks between North Vietnam and the United States
   c. the forced resignation of French President Charles de Gaulle
   d. the signing of the Evian Accords granting independence to Algeria

3. In a 1963 treaty, the United States, Great Britain, and the Soviet Union promised
   a. not to test nuclear weapons in the atmosphere or under the sea
   b. to divide Berlin into two separate sectors
   c. not to intercede militarily in Asian affairs
   d. not to use nuclear weapons in case of global war

4. The Warren Commission found that the assassination of President John F. Kennedy
   a. had been carried out by a lone gunman
   b. had been the work of a conspiracy involving organized crime

   c. had been planned and executed by a network of Cuban refugees

   d. none of the above

Ron Galella, Ltd.

5. With which of the following policies was this man *not* associated?

   a. initiating the secret U.S. bombing of Cambodia

   b. returning the shah to power in Iran

   c. escalating the secret war in Laos

   d. overthrowing President Salvador Allende in Chile

6. In the 1960s the United States and the Soviet Union competed for influence most actively

   a. in the countries of Western Europe

   b. in the countries of Central and Eastern Europe

   c. in the countries along the Soviet border

   d. in the developing countries

AP / Wide World Photos

7. For what was this person chiefly known?

   a. leading the Chinese Communist party from 1935 to 1976

   b. overthrowing the Chinese emperor and establishing a republic

   c. leading the movement for Vietnamese independence

   d. serving as president of South Vietnam from 1967 to 1975

8. During the Asian holiday of Tet in 1968,

   a. Buddhist monks set themselves on fire in protest against the South Vietnamese government

   b. Soviet and Chinese soldiers exchanged artillery fire along the Manchurian border

   c. the Viet Cong launched surprise attacks throughout South Vietnam

   d. Ferdinand Marcos was elected president of the Philippines

9. What was the War on Poverty?

 a. a series of antipoverty programs enacted under the Johnson administration

 b. the Johnson administration's "Marshall Plan" for the developing countries

 c. President Kennedy's plan to aid the poorer nations of Latin America

 d. a 1964 program in which college students volunteered to teach job skills to ghetto residents

10. The Peace Corps was established in 1961 with the aim of

 a. providing on-the-spot aid and instruction to third-world people

 b. providing counterinsurgency training to third-world allies

 c. teaching American values to foreign university students

 d. patrolling crisis areas and preventing the outbreak of war

11. Which of the following men was assassinated on November 2, 1963?

 a. President Syngman Rhee of South Korea

 b. U.S. President John F. Kennedy

 c. Frederick Nolting, U.S. ambassador to South Vietnam

 d. President Ngo Dinh Diem of South Vietnam

12. What happened in 1961 at a place called the Bay of Pigs?

 a. U.S.-sponsored Cuban exiles attempted to invade Cuba.

 b. Indonesian Communists rebelled against President Sukarno.

    c. Cuban Communist guerrillas attacked the Moncada barracks.

    d. Communist insurgents in Malaya were defeated by British-led troops.

13. At the time of his assassination, Robert F. Kennedy was

    a. attorney general of the United States

    b. running for the Democratic presidential nomination

    c. the Democratic nominee for president

    d. U.S. senator from Massachusetts

14. The first person to orbit the earth in a spacecraft was

    a. Yuri Gagarin, in 1961

    b. Alan Shepard, in 1961

    c. Gherman Titov, in 1961

    d. John Glenn, in 1962

15. In 1970 the Communist Khmer Rouge forces in Cambodia

    a. were defeated and routed by invading U.S. troops

    b. agreed to a temporary alliance with the South Vietnamese

    c. began a war to overthrow the U.S.-backed regime of Lon Nol

    d. proclaimed their allegiance to Prince Norodom Sihanouk

16. What was the "Prague Spring" in Czechoslovakia in 1968?

    a. the ouster of Communist party leader Alexander Dubček

    b. an experiment in democratic reform

    c. a series of purges that consolidated Communist rule

    d. a rash of violent strikes by industrial workers

17. Which countries joined the "club" of nuclear powers during the 1960s?

a. the Soviet Union and China

b. India and Japan

c. China and France

d. France and Great Britain

18. Who were the victims of the 1960 Sharpeville Massacre?

a. striking coal miners in western Pennsylvania

b. English railway workers protesting a lockout by the government

c. Catholics in Northern Ireland protesting British rule

d. South African blacks protesting the "pass" laws

19. In 1967, Nguyen Van Thieu and Nguyen Cao Ky

a. became president and vice-president of South Vietnam

b. led a coup that toppled the Vietnamese emperor Bao Dai

c. represented Vietnam's National Liberation Front at the Paris peace talks

d. accepted cabinet posts in Vietnam's Provisional Revolutionary Government

20. Salvador Allende was the first

a. right-wing dictator in Chilean history

b. South American leader to recognize the Castro government

c. of two Argentine presidents overthrown by Juan Perón

d. freely elected Marxist president in the Western Hemisphere

21. What was Biafra?

    a. a party of South African blacks that challenged apartheid in the 1960s

    b. a region that seceded from Nigeria in 1967

    c. the name for Ghana before it became independent from Great Britain

    d. the organization of African countries founded by Kwame Nkrumah

22. What happened in the 1968 *Pueblo* incident?

    a. A Cuban gunboat was hijacked to Florida.

    b. An Argentine battleship shelled a British base in the Falklands.

    c. A U.S. warship was seized by North Korea.

    d. A Mexican tanker was hijacked to Cuba.

23. In the Vietnam War, the Vietnamese General Vo Nguyen Giap proved himself to be

    a. a hero in the U.S. and South Vietnamese cause

    b. a failure in the methods of counterinsurgency

    c. a genius in the tactics of hit-and-run guerrilla warfare

    d. interested only in personal advancement while the war effort deteriorated

24. In his "Great Society" speech (1964), President Lyndon Johnson promised

    a. a society free of prejudice and poverty

    b. a society free of the threat of nuclear annihilation

    c. a society in which there would be no cause for political dissent

    d. a society free of the need to import foreign oil

25. General William Westmoreland was the officer in Vietnam who was responsible for

   a. ordering the attack on My Lai

   b. leading the Green Berets

   c. representing the United States in peace negotiations

   d. commanding all U.S. troops

26. The Cuban missile crisis revolved around

   a. an atom bomb developed by Cuban scientists

   b. Soviet missiles deployed in Cuba

   c. missiles launched against Cuban airliners by Cuban exiles based in Florida

   d. Soviet missiles aimed at Cuba

27. Which countries fought in the Six-Day War of 1967?

   a. Israel, Lebanon, and Iraq

   b. Greece and Turkey

   c. China and North Vietnam

   d. Israel, Egypt, Syria, and Jordan

28. The Berlin Wall was erected in 1961 in response to

   a. the Soviet military threat to West Berlin

   b. the flight of East Germans to West Berlin

   c. the threat of NATO forces to Eastern Europe

   d. the Berlin airlift

29. What did the events of May 1968 in France seem to demonstrate?

   a. that any threat to European security would be put down by force

   b. that students were the only group capable of leading a rebellion

   c. that a leftist revolt was still possible in an advanced industrial country

   d. that revolution was impossible in Western Europe

30. The Great Cultural Revolution in China in the late 1960s aimed to
  a. imitate the best features of Western culture
  b. increase national pride in Chinese art, music, and dance
  c. revitalize the people's revolutionary spirit
  d. open cultural exchanges with the Soviet Union

31. In which of its colonies did France wage a full-scale war during the late 1950s and early 1960s?
  a. Senegal
  b. Algeria
  c. Chad
  d. Ivory Coast

32. The Tonkin Gulf resolution adopted by Congress in 1964 allowed President Johnson to
  a. send U.S. troops to Vietnam without a declaration of war
  b. initiate contacts with the Chinese government
  c. advance U.S. forces in Vietnam as far as the Chinese border
  d. request the SEATO allies to send troops to Vietnam

33. Active U.S. participation in the Vietnam War ended
  a. only when Saigon fell in 1975
  b. with a cease-fire in 1973
  c. with Operation Homecoming in 1973
  d. with the resignation of President Richard Nixon in 1974

34. How did African decolonization in the 1960s help shape politics in America?
  a. The dismantling of the European empires influenced U.S. policy in Latin America.

    b. The violence against African blacks encouraged white violence against blacks in the United States.

    c. The left-wing sympathies of many of the new countries led to the withholding of all American aid.

    d. The success of African independence movements encouraged the growing black civil rights movement.

35. What was the main function of the Ho Chi Minh Trail?

    a. It was the highway to Hanoi for troop convoys from China.

    b. It was the main road to Laos for Soviet supply trucks.

    c. It was a transport route southward for military supplies from North Vietnam.

    d. It was the coast road used nightly by Viet Cong couriers.

36. The Tupamaros were Marxist rebels who in the 1960s waged guerrilla war in

    a. Argentina

    b. Honduras

    c. Venezuela

    d. Uruguay

37. In 1965 in Indonesia,

    a. the government voted to send troops to fight in South Vietnam

    b. half a million suspected Communists were killed following an army coup

    c. a nationalist guerrilla movement took up arms against Dutch rule

    d. Communist guerrillas began an insurrection against President Sukarno

38. With what crime was First Lieutenant William Calley charged in Vietnam in 1968?

   a. murdering Vietnamese civilians at My Lai

   b. distributing heroin to the soldiers under his command

   c. deserting during the Tet offensive

   d. giving antiwar speeches on Hanoi radio

39. Which of the following countries did *not* have mass student protests in 1968?

   a. West Germany

   b. Italy

   c. Japan

   d. Portugal

40. Which of the following helped lead the movement to end British rule in Northern Ireland?

   a. Ian Paisley

   b. Daniel Cohn-Bendit

   c. Bernadette Devlin

   d. Bernardine Dohrn

TEST 2: Explanatory Answers

1. **(d)** The Viet Cong were Communist insurgents in South Vietnam who, starting in 1956, waged a guerrilla war against the U.S.-backed government. They were also known by the name of their political organization, the National Liberation Front (NLF). Aided by Communist North Vietnam, by the early 1960s they controlled almost half of the country. In 1961, however, U.S. troops entered the war to bolster the government, and thereafter the fighting steadily escalated. U.S. forces grew to 200,000 and later to more than 500,000, while the Viet Cong were reinforced by North Vietnamese troops. Massive U.S. bombing raids were directed against insurgent strongholds and, after 1965, against North Vietnam. Yet the Americans, despite their vast military superiority, never inflicted a decisive defeat on the Viet Cong and their allies. Indeed, after the insurgents' Tet offensive in 1968, many Americans concluded that the war was unwinnable. In 1969 the NLF was invited to join the Paris peace talks, and in 1973 the NLF's Provisional Revolutionary Government (PRG) was among the signers of the peace agreement. After the fall of South Vietnam in 1975, NLF representatives were included in the government of reunited Vietnam.

2. **(b)** In May 1968, just as antigovernment demonstrations and strikes by students and workers were bringing France to a standstill, peace talks opened in Paris between North Vietnam and the United States. The talks, begun after President Lyndon Johnson decided not to seek reelection, dragged on for years thereafter, with Henry Kissinger as chief negotiator for the Nixon administration. Only in 1973, after four more years of warfare and massive U.S. bombing in Vietnam, was a peace agreement at last achieved.

3. **(a)** This first Nuclear Test-Ban Treaty, signed on August 5, 1963, banned tests in outer space, in the atmosphere, and under the sea. At the time of the treaty, only four countries had nuclear weapons; France did not sign and continued testing in the atmosphere over the Pacific Ocean.

4. **(a)** The assassination of John F. Kennedy on November 22, 1963, and the murder, two days later, of Lee Harvey Oswald, the suspected gunman, led the new president, Lyndon B.

Johnson, to appoint an official commission of inquiry. Headed by Chief Justice Earl Warren, the commission conducted hearings that culminated in a report issued on September 24, 1964. The commission concluded that Oswald had acted alone. However, later congressional committee hearings led to a different conclusion: acoustical evidence, it was decided, proved the existence of two gunmen. Yet this finding too has been disputed, and the Warren Commission's report remains generally accepted.

5. **(b)** Henry Kissinger was national security advisor to President Richard Nixon until 1973 and then secretary of state under Nixon and Gerald Ford. The secret bombing of Cambodia was begun shortly after the Nixon administration came to power; and in Laos, secret operations (mainly bombing of the Ho Chi Minh Trail) were greatly escalated. The leftist President Salvador Allende of Chile was overthrown in 1973 in an army coup backed by the CIA and approved by Kissinger's State Department. The Iran episode, in which the CIA returned the shah to power after the ouster of a militant nationalist government, took place in 1953.

6. **(d)** The developing countries of Asia, Africa, the Caribbean, and Latin America—many newly independent after the dismantling of the European colonial empires—were the main focus of U.S.–Soviet rivalry in the 1960s as each superpower tried to secure its strategic interests in these areas. In many of these countries, the Soviets backed nationalist, often leftist guerrillas fighting to overthrow local ruling elites—land-owning classes, European-educated governing classes, and the like—who were often supported by the United States. These third-world rebel movements, with their revolutionary rhetoric and leftist aspirations that often owed more to Mao than to Marx, provided numerous heroes for the American New Left.

7. **(c)** Ho Chi Minh (c. 1890–1969) was the pseudonym of Nguyen That Thanh, the founder in 1930 of the Communist party of Indochina. In the 1940s and 1950s, he led the struggle for independence from France; his followers in that period were known as the Viet Minh. When Vietnam was partitioned in 1954, Ho was named president of North Vietnam. He served in that capacity until his death in 1969, sending aid and eventually North Vietnamese troops to support the Communist Viet Cong in South Vietnam in their struggle against the

South Vietnamese government and the U.S. troops that defended it. After Ho's death, Ton Duc Thang became president of North Vietnam. The wrong answers describe Mao Zedong, Sun Yat Sen, and Nguyen Van Thieu.

8. **(c)** Tet, the Vietnamese New Year, was supposed to be a ceasefire period throughout Vietnam. However, on January 30, 1968, the Viet Cong and North Vietnamese troops launched surprise attacks on more than thirty South Vietnamese provincial capitals. They temporarily captured Hue, and in Saigon they penetrated as far as the grounds of the U.S. embassy. After heavy fighting, the insurgents were forced to retreat, suffering enormous casualties. Nevertheless, for them the Tet offensive was a kind of victory, for it proved that they were still capable of attacking virtually anywhere in South Vietnam, thus giving the lie to official U.S. reports of their imminent defeat. For many in the United States, the Tet offensive was the moment when they concluded that the war was unwinnable; the antiwar movement was greatly strengthened, and just a few months later, President Johnson announced his decision not to seek reelection.

9. **(a)** Lyndon Johnson's War on Poverty reforms began with the Economic Opportunity Act of 1964. This and other acts established a whole series of antipoverty programs, including job training, expanded loans to businesses in depressed areas, legal-aid services to the poor, school lunch programs, and dozens of other services.

10. **(a)** Established in 1961 under President John F. Kennedy and still flourishing, the Peace Corps sends young volunteers to third-world countries to provide on-the-spot training in farming, health care, and education. In the 1960s, the Corps appealed to many countercultural types because of its promise of an alternative, altruistic lifestyle. Reality was another matter, however, and in the early years volunteers sometimes made serious blunders and in a few cases were asked to leave their host countries.

11. **(d)** President Ngo Dinh Diem was president of the U.S.-backed government of South Vietnam starting in 1955. He was reelected in 1961, but his army failed to stem the Viet Cong rebels, and his authoritarian rule provoked resentment among the civilian population. A crisis arose in May 1963 when seven

Buddhist monks immolated themselves to protest government persecution. When antigovernment demonstrations followed, army commanders—with the approval of the Kennedy administration—staged a coup. During the fighting, Diem and his brother Ngo Dinh Nhu, the head of the secret police, were assassinated.

12. **(a)** The CIA and the Eisenhower administration had planned the invasion of Cuba in 1960. On taking over in 1961, Kennedy approved the plan, which proposed to drop a force of 1,500 Cubans on the southern coast of Cuba to spark an internal rebellion. The mission failed miserably, partly because Kennedy did not supply air cover and perhaps because the United States underestimated Fidel Castro's support in Cuba. More than 1,000 invaders were captured and later ransomed back to the United States in return for several million dollars' worth of food and medicine.

13. **(b)** Robert F. Kennedy (1925–1968) served as attorney general of the United States from 1961 to 1964. He was elected senator from New York in 1964 and ran for the Democratic presidential nomination in the 1968 election. Following his victory speech after the California primary on June 5, he was shot by Sirhan Sirhan, a twenty-four-year-old Jordanian, reportedly angered by Kennedy's support of Israel. Kennedy died the next day.

14. **(a)** From the time the Soviet *Sputnik* satellite was launched in 1957, the Soviet Union and the United States were engaged in a new arena of the cold war: the space race. The Soviet cosmonaut Yuri Gagarin orbited the earth inside *Vostok I* on April 12, 1961; in 1962 John Glenn was the first American to orbit the earth. The Soviet Union's Aleksei Leonov was the first man to walk in space, in March 1965; Edward White did so for the United States three months later. By the late 1960s the Soviets were concentrating less on manned space flight. Neil Armstrong walked on the moon in 1969; one year later an unmanned Soviet moon probe landed on the moon and returned to earth.

15. **(c)** In 1970, just prior to a U.S.–South Vietnamese invasion of Cambodia, the neutralist Cambodian government of Prince Norodom Sihanouk was ousted by a group of U.S.-backed generals in a coup said to have CIA support. General Lon Nol headed a new regime, but his forces soon came under attack from the Cambodian Communist guerrillas called the Khmer Rouge. Fighting steadily escalated, and even though the government received massive U.S. aid, in 1975 the rebels seized the capital, Phnom Penh. Immediately after their victory, the Khmer Rouge and their leader, Pol Pot, instituted a reign of terror: virtually the whole population was sent to labor in the countryside under brutal conditions, and up to three million perished. In 1978–1979 Vietnam invaded Cambodia and forced the Khmer Rouge leaders to seek refuge in Thailand; however, Vietnam's scheduled withdrawal by 1990 left the future situation uncertain.

16. (b) In late 1967, a violent crackdown by Czech police on student protestors spurred calls for change, and in January 1968 the country's ruling Communist party, led by the moderate Alexander Dubček, purged its hard-liners and initiated major reforms of the country's political and economic systems. This period of free speech and democratic renewal was dubbed the Prague Spring. It ended the following August when Soviet-led Warsaw Pact troops invaded the country under the pretext of averting a counterrevolution. Most of the new policies were overturned, and Dubček was later ousted. While it lasted, the Prague Spring was an inspiration to those around the world who dreamed of democratic reforms and a humane Socialist alternative to Soviet-style communism.

17. (c) The United States was the first country to develop atomic weapons and is the only one ever to use them in war. By 1959, two more countries had developed atomic bombs: the Soviet Union and Great Britain. France built its first atomic bomb in 1960, followed by China in 1964 and India in 1974.

18. (d) In 1960 at Sharpeville, near Johannesburg, protesters organized by the African National Congress were demonstrating peacefully against the "pass" laws—onerous regulations designed to restrict blacks' freedom to travel around the country—when troops opened fire. Approximately 70 demonstrators were killed and another 190 were wounded.

19. (a) Following the overthrow and murder in 1963 of South Vietnam's president, Ngo Dinh Diem, the country was governed by a series of military councils. In June 1965, General Nguyen Van Thieu became head of state, and Air Vice-Marshal Nguyen Cao Ky became prime minister. With U.S. backing, a new constitution was drafted, providing for a strong executive; in 1967 Thieu and Ky were elected president and vice-president, respectively. In 1971, Thieu was reelected unopposed, and he gradually assumed dictatorial power. In 1975, when Saigon at last fell to the Communist forces, both Thieu and Ky fled to the United States.

20. **(d)** Salvador Allende Gossens (1908–1973), head of the Chilean Socialist party, was elected president of Chile in 1970. He nationalized Chile's important copper industry and instituted various Socialist programs, but strikes in 1972 caused him to impose martial law. After one unsuccessful attempt, the military overthrew Allende in 1973, and he was killed during the coup. Ever since, General Augusto Pinochet Ugarto's right-wing dictatorship has been in power. The role of the U.S. State Department and the CIA in fomenting strikes, destabilizing the government, and ousting Allende was made public in the mid-1970s.

21. **(b)** Fearing continued massacres by Muslim Hausas, Ibo separatists seceded from Nigeria in 1967 and founded the state of Biafra. War broke out soon afterward, and Biafra was defeated in 1970. During the war, more than one million Biafrans starved to death.

22. **(c)** The navy intelligence ship *Pueblo* and its crew of eighty-three were captured off the coast of North Korea on January 23, 1968. North Korea said that the ship had intruded on its territory and insisted on receiving an apology; the United States insisted that the ship was in international waters. The crew was held for nearly a year before an apology was issued. North Korea was an ally of North Vietnam; some suspected that the seizure was a decoy to throw the United States off the scent of the upcoming Tet offensive.

23. **(c)** General Vo Nguyen Giap of North Vietnam is credited with masterminding the hit-and-run tactics of jungle guerrilla warfare that eventually brought victory to the Communist forces in Vietnam. It was in response to Giap's strategies that the United States developed the whole range of specialized counterinsurgency techniques used by the Green Berets and others. Giap occupied a place close to Che Guevara in the American New Left's pantheon of heroes.

24. **(a)** President Lyndon Johnson's "Great Society" slogan was the brainchild of speechwriter Richard Goodwin. The speech that presented the idea was given in May 1964. Johnson spoke about the capacity of Americans to use their wealth and abundant resources to build a society free from prejudice and poverty, in which every person would have the opportunity to lead a happy and fulfilling life.

25. **(d)** Starting in 1960, William Westmoreland, then an army major general, served as superintendent general at West Point. In 1964, President Lyndon Johnson needed a new commander in Vietnam, and he named Westmoreland. Westmoreland commanded all U.S. troops in Vietnam until 1968, and his aggressive strategies did much to shape the course of the war.

26. **(b)** In October 1962, U.S. reconnaissance discovered nuclear-armed Soviet missiles in Cuba. The Soviets claimed that the missiles were there to protect Cuba from attack, but President Kennedy demanded that they be removed and imposed a naval blockade around Cuba to bar further Soviet missile shipments. After a week in which all-out nuclear war appeared imminent, the Soviets agreed to a compromise in which they would remove their missiles from Cuba in return for the removal of U.S. missiles from Turkey.

27. **(d)** In May 1967, President Gamal Abdel Nasser of Egypt responded to growing Arab–Israeli tension by blockading Israel's sea routes through the Gulf of Aqaba and by removing the UN peacekeeping force in the Sinai. Israel then launched attacks against Egypt, Jordan, and Syria. In six days (June 5–10), Israel conquered the Sinai Peninsula, the Gaza Strip, the Jordanian West Bank, and the eastern sector of Jerusalem. All but the Sinai are still under Israeli control.

28. **(b)** After World War II, Berlin was split into West Berlin, eventually a part of West Germany, and East Berlin, which became the capital of East Germany. Until 1961 passage between the two was not tightly controlled, and West Berlin attracted many thousands of East German refugees. Then in August 1961 the East Germans sealed off the border by erecting a 39-mile wall patrolled by armed guards. The Wall became a potent symbol of the East–West cold war split.

29. **(c)** The events of 1968 in France arose from protests in 1967 at the suburban Nanterre campus of the University of Paris, where students rebelled against the outdated, repressive national education system. The following spring the demonstrations spread to the Sorbonne in Paris, where students fought a series of violent street battles with the police. Events then quickly escalated. The brutality of the police led middle- and working-class people to support the student cause, and demonstrations in Paris and around the country soon turned into mass rallies against the government of President Charles de Gaulle. Support strikes broke out and spread swiftly to the factories, railroads, the national television network, and even farms; and by the end of May some ten million people were on strike, bringing France to a halt. At that point de Gaulle, blaming the Communist party for the crisis, dissolved the national assembly, called for new elections, and put the army on alert. In the elections, de Gaulle and his party won a great victory, and thereafter the strike movement lost its momentum. Nevertheless, to youthful revolutionaries everywhere, the lesson was clear: full-scale revolution was still possible in the advanced industrial countries.

30. **(c)** The Great Cultural Revolution that began in China in 1966 was essentially a power struggle between Mao Zedong and "revisionist" Communist party officials whom he dubbed "capitalist roaders." To help him in this struggle, Mao enlisted the Chinese people and attempted to rekindle their revolutionary spirit with a campaign to eradicate all vestiges of capitalism and bourgeois culture. Political tests were applied to officials and ordinary citizens; those who failed were imprisoned or sent to hard labor in reeducation camps or in the countryside. Young people, organized as revolutionary Red Guards, fought pitched battles in city streets against those branded as counterrevolutionaries. Only after violence and disorder had almost paralyzed the country was the campaign ended.

31. **(b)** In 1954, French rule in Algeria was challenged by a nationalist revolt led by the radical National Liberation Front (FLN). French troops put down the revolt in the cities, but guerrilla fighting erupted in the countryside. The war went on until the early 1960s, when the French government of Charles de Gaulle at last recognized that independence for Algeria was inevitable. An accord granting independence was finally reached in 1962. During the course of the war, there were numerous protests against it in France; these strongly influenced the later protests in the United States against the Vietnam War.

32. **(a)** In 1964 in the Gulf of Tonkin off North Vietnam, two U.S. destroyers reported that they had been fired on by North Vietnamese gunboats. President Lyndon Johnson then asked sixteen congressional leaders for a resolution allowing him to take whatever action he considered necessary to respond to the alleged attack. All sixteen approved the resolution, and it passed unanimously in the House and with only two opposing votes in the Senate. In the years that followed, this resolution remained the legal basis for sending U.S. troops to South Vietnam and for bombing North Vietnam, all without an actual declaration of war.

33. **(b)** Even though peace talks between the United States and North Vietnam began in Paris in 1968, it took five years to reach an agreement. Henry Kissinger, President Richard Nixon's representative, spent several years negotiating with Le Duc Tho, North Vietnam's envoy; then in 1972 progress stopped while the United States subjected Hanoi to saturation bombing. Finally, on January 23, 1973, a cease-fire agreement was signed, and soon afterward most U.S. troops were withdrawn. The United States took no further part in the fighting in Vietnam, and the U.S. presence ended completely with the fall of Saigon in 1975.

34. **(d)** As countries in Africa achieved independence from the European powers, blacks in the United States took increasing pride in their African heritage. Having a successful freedom movement with which to identify lent strength and new meaning to the struggle for blacks' civil rights in the United States.

35. **(c)** The Ho Chi Minh Trail was actually a series of trails and jungle roadways leading from North Vietnam through Laos to the Communist-controlled areas of South Vietnam. Throughout the Vietnam War it was used as a transport route for North Vietnamese supplies and troops being sent to aid the Communist insurgency in South Vietnam. Regularly bombed by the U.S. Air Force, it was repaired each night by the Vietnamese; it has been estimated that traffic on the Trail increased steadily despite the bombing.

36. **(d)** The Tupamaro National Liberation Front was a group of leftist guerrillas who carried out terrorist attacks and guerrilla warfare in Uruguay in the 1960s and early 1970s. Many were university-educated but unable to find jobs in the country's stagnant economy. By the mid-1970s the army had arrested most of the rebels; many were subjected to torture. The Tupamaros were another of the third-world revolutionary bands admired by American New Leftists in the 1960s.

37. **(b)** In 1965 in Indonesia, conservatives in the army suspected that the country's Communists were planning a coup with the tacit support of the country's charismatic leader, President Sukarno. To forestall this possibility, the army itself staged a coup, replacing Sukarno with a conservative military government. In the weeks that followed, perhaps half a million suspected Communists were rounded up and massacred. These events reflected the pattern of Communist insurgencies and conservative counterattacks then common in so much of Southeast Asia.

38. **(a)** On March 6, 1968, Lieutenant Calley and his troops murdered more than one hundred civilians in the South Vietnamese town of My Lai. Efforts were made to cover up the incident, but in the end Calley was put on trial. He eventually served just three years under house arrest.

39. **(d)** The year 1968 saw mass student demonstrations in the United States, Eastern and Western Europe, and many other places. France, Poland, Italy, Czechoslovakia, Japan, Spain, Great Britain, West Germany, Belgium, Yugoslavia, Mexico, and Ireland were all scenes of student protests against outmoded curricula and government repression.

40. **(c)** Bernadette Devlin was a member of People's Democracy, one of many mostly Catholic Northern Ireland groups opposed to British rule. In 1969 she was elected to the British Parliament and became a media sensation because of her leftist leanings and blunt criticisms of British policies. On January 30, 1972 ("Bloody Sunday"), British troops attacked marchers in Belfast, and thirteen Catholics were killed. The following day, Devlin physically attacked British Home Secretary Reginald Maudling on the floor of the House of Commons, for which she was later jailed.

Hell No, We Won't Go: Politics and Protest

What is a rebel?
A man who says no.

—*ALBERT CAMUS*

1. Which of the following people was *not* one of the Chicago Seven?

   a. Jerry Rubin

   b. Tom Hayden

   c. Mario Savio

   d. Rennie Davis

2. Who were the Boston Five?

   a. SDS protesters who were arrested for occupying a building at Boston University in 1969

   b. underground journalists who were accused of leaking classified information to the *Boston Globe* in 1971

   c. protest leaders who were indicted for antidraft activities

   d. radical Harvard professors who were fired for supporting SDS demands

3. Why was the Dow Chemical Company such a frequent target of 1960s student protests?

   a. It refused to hire women as research scientists.

   b. Its manufacturing operations produced toxic chemical wastes.

   c. Its president was a vocal supporter of the Vietnam War.

   d. It manufactured a chemical weapon used in Vietnam.

4. *Revolution for the Hell of It* was written by "Free." What was the author's real name?

a. Abbie Hoffman

b. Jerry Rubin

c. Tom Hayden

d. Jack Kerouac

5. Which of the following is a major way in which the New Left differed from the Old Left?

a. It advocated using violence to force social change.

b. It believed in using democratic methods to reach political solutions.

c. It considered the working class to be the vanguard of a Socialist revolution.

d. It called for strict adherence to the philosophies of Marx and Lenin.

6. What happened when a young man "won" the draft lottery?

    a. He received a cash prize.

    b. He was given a very high number.

    c. He burned his draft card.

    d. He was given a very low number.

7. What was the Spring Mobilization's greatest success?

    a. the April 1967 mass demonstrations against the war

    b. the defense of the Catonsville Nine

    c. the release of Huey Newton from prison in California

    d. the spring 1969 strike at Harvard University

8. What sparked the October 1965 mass march from Berkeley to Oakland?

    a. the university rule against speechmaking on the Berkeley campus

    b. President Johnson's bombing of North Vietnam in reprisal for the Tonkin Gulf incident

    c. the racist attitudes of the Oakland police force

    d. the arrival of General William Westmoreland at an Oakland army base

9. What was the purpose of the group called the Resistance?

    a. to organize civil disobedience inside the armed forces

    b. to use violence to protect antiwar demonstrators

    c. to help those who refused conscription

    d. to bomb institutions that symbolized U.S. imperialism

10. What happened to the Black Panther leader Fred Hampton on December 4, 1969?

   a. He was shot and killed by the Chicago police.

   b. He was elected to the Berkeley city council.

   c. He was acquitted of the charge of conspiring to disrupt the Democratic National Convention.

   d. He broke out of prison and fled to Algeria.

11. Which of the following groups carried out a moving antiwar demonstration on the steps of the U.S. Capitol?

   a. the Yippies

   b. the New Frontier

   c. the Vietnam Veterans Against the War

   d. the War Resisters League

12. What happened at Kent State University in Ohio on May 4, 1970?

   a. The ROTC building was burned down.

   b. Four students were shot and killed by the National Guard.

   c. Two students were killed by a bomb placed by the Weather Underground.

   d. Students held the university president hostage for forty-eight hours.

13. According to polls, most Americans who came to oppose the Vietnam War did so because

   a. they considered the war immoral

   b. they feared the war's brutality was corrupting American soldiers

   c. they were concerned about the suffering of the Vietnamese

   d. they considered the war unwinnable and too costly in American lives

14. When SDS was first launched in 1960, what was its main goal?

   a. to build a society based on "participatory democracy"

   b. to reform university curricula

   c. to overthrow the government of the United States

   d. to end the war in Vietnam

15. At which university did the 1964 Free Speech Movement take place?

   a. University of Michigan at Ann Arbor

   b. Cornell University

   c. Columbia University

   d. University of California at Berkeley

16. What group secretly influenced the National Student Association during the early 1960s?

   a. SDS

   b. the CIA

   c. the FBI

   d. the NLF

17. The radical group called the Weathermen were originally a faction of

   a. SDS

   b. the Progressive Labor Party

   c. the White Panthers

   d. the Yippies

18. The leftist activist Kathy Boudin became famous as

   a. the woman who became leader of the Weathermen and renamed the organization the Weather Underground

   b. a fugitive wanted in the accidental blowing up of a New York City town house

    c. the organizer of a month-long sit-in at Harvard University

    d. the head of a Marxist group that disrupted classes at the University of Chicago

19. Who were the Berrigans?

    a. a folk-rock group who performed at peace rallies

    b. Catholic priests who were jailed for protesting the Vietnam War

    c. a Yippie couple who sheltered draft dodgers

    d. editors of the underground *Los Angeles Free Press*

20. Where and when did the Days of Rage demonstrations take place?

    a. during the 1968 Democratic convention in Chicago

    b. during the 1970 trial of Bobby Seale in New Haven

    c. in New York following the U.S. Christmas bombing of Hanoi in 1972

    d. during the 1969 trial of the Chicago Seven in Chicago

21. Of what organization was Tom Hayden the president?

    a. Students for a Democratic Society

    b. Americans for Democratic Action

    c. Student League for Industrial Democracy

    d. Fellowship of Reconciliation

22. Student antiwar protesters rioted in 1970 and burned down a bank building in

    a. Ann Arbor, Michigan

    b. San Jose, California

    c. Madison, Wisconsin

    d. Santa Barbara, California

23. Which of these bombings by leftist radicals resulted in fatalities?

    a. the bombing of IBM headquarters in New York City

    b. the bombing of the University of Wisconsin's army mathematics research building

    c. the bombing of Mobil headquarters in New York City

    d. the bombing of the U.S. Senate offices

24. What happened in the 1969 Stonewall Riot?

    a. workers rebelled against the Dow Chemical Company

    b. a Detroit ghetto was burned to the ground

    c. a gay bar in Greenwich Village was raided by police

    d. student protesters were set upon by hardhats

25. Mark Rudd first became famous as

    a. the spokesperson for the Young People's Socialist League

    b. a leader of Columbia's student uprising

    c. the founder of the Free Speech movement

    d. the first draftee to burn his draft card

26. What happened at Jackson State College in Mississippi in 1970?

    a. National Guardsmen shot and killed student protesters.

    b. A student strike ended with the permanent closing of the school.

    c. ROTC cadets and black students fought the Battle of the Quad.

    d. Vice President Nguyen Cao Ky of South Vietnam was stoned by student demonstrators.

27. Who were the Catonsville Nine?

    a. demonstrators arrested for blockading a weapons factory in Tennessee

    b. Catholics arrested for burning draft records in Maryland

    c. students arrested for disrupting a Hubert Humphrey campaign appearance in Virginia

    d. Vietnam veterans arrested outside a North Carolina military facility

28. Which of the following ideas was *not* proposed by the Yippies in 1968?

    a. running a pig for president

    b. spiking the Chicago water supply with LSD

    c. seducing politicians and their wives

    d. erecting a tent city on the Mall in Washington

29. What was the Mobe?

    a. the National Mobilization Committee to End the War in Vietnam

    b. shorthand for the Johnson administration's plan to bomb North Vietnam

    c. a radical newspaper published by students at Berkeley

    d. a loose-knit underground organization whose purpose was to bail out arrested protesters

30. What was the Venceremos Brigade?

    a. a band of students sworn to avenge the murder of Che Guevara

    b. Puerto Rican nationalists seeking independence for their homeland

    c. California radicals organized into an "affinity group" for streetfighting

    d. a group of volunteers who helped cut sugar cane in Cuba

31. The Progressive Labor party
   a. nominated Angela Davis for president in 1968
   b. infiltrated and took over the national SDS organization in 1969
   c. staged "disruptive happenings" in Chicago in 1968
   d. founded a university for factory workers in Detroit

32. Bernardine Dohrn was a leader of
   a. the Resistance
   b. the Free Speech Movement
   c. the Weather Underground
   d. Women's Strike for Peace

33. What was the Moratorium of November 1969?
   a. a one-month work stoppage by university-affiliated weapons researchers
   b. a ten-day student blockade of the Oakland induction center
   c. a nationwide antiwar strike
   d. a four-day shutdown of Harvard University in protest against the war

34. Which of the following events did *not* occur during the 1968 Chicago Democratic convention?
   a. Black delegates walked out when the nearly all-white Alabama delegation was seated.
   b. A campaign to draft Ted Kennedy was begun.
   c. A police riot took place in the streets of the city.
   d. A peace plank was added to the party platform.

35. Which of these people was *not* a member of SDS?
   a. Rennie Davis
   b. Tom Hayden
   c. Bobby Seale
   d. Todd Gitlin

36. At the time he ran for president, Eugene McCarthy was
    a. an anti-Communist senator from Wisconsin
    b. an antiwar senator from Minnesota
    c. provost of the University of Chicago
    d. senior aide to Allard K. Lowenstein

37. The "Free Huey" movement aimed to
    a. release the Chicago Seven from prison
    b. reverse the murder conviction of a Black Panther leader
    c. make the government drop charges against a leading Weatherman
    d. prove SDS's first president innocent of bombing charges

Bernie Boston

38. Where did the event shown take place?
    a. at the March on the Pentagon in 1967
    b. during the Democratic National convention in 1968

    c. during a parade celebrating the end of the Vietnam War

    d. at Kent State University in 1970

39. About how many draft evaders were reported between 1966 and 1970?

    a. 10,000

    b. 25,000

    c. 50,000

    d. 150,000

40. A comedian known for his support of civil rights and the antiwar movement was

    a. Bob Hope

    b. Red Skelton

    c. Bill Cosby

    d. Dick Gregory

TEST 3: Explanatory Answers

1. **(c)** Mario Savio was a leader of the Free Speech Movement in Berkeley in 1964. The Chicago Seven, tried for their part in the protests at the 1968 Chicago Democratic Convention, included Jerry Rubin and Abbie Hoffman of the Yippies; Tom Hayden, Rennie Davis, and David Dellinger of the Mobe; and protesters John Froines and Lee Weiner. Bobby Seale of the Black Panthers was originally indicted with the others—the original trial was to be of the "Chicago Eight"—but his trial was separated from the joint trial of the others. The co-defendants were acquitted of conspiracy charges, but Rubin, Hoffman, Hayden, Davis, and Dellinger were convicted of lesser charges. Their convictions were overturned in 1972.

2. **(c)** On October 16, 1967, at a public demonstration in Boston, fifty young men burned their draft cards, and the Boston Five—William Sloane Coffin, Benjamin Spock, Michael Ferber, Mitchell Goodman, and Marcus Raskin—collected the cards of 250 others. The Reverend Mr. Coffin took the cards to the Justice Department in Washington, which refused to accept them, and the five were indicted on charges of conspiracy. They were later acquitted.

3. **(d)** The Dow Chemical Company manufactured a chemical weapon called napalm, a sort of jellied gasoline used in flamethrowers and dropped in bombs. Used freely by the American forces in Vietnam, it caused frightful burns on its victims, many of them civilians. In consequence, the company was a favorite target of antiwar protesters; visits to campuses by Dow recruiters were frequently met with demonstrations and sit-ins.

4. **(a)** Abbie Hoffman (1936–1989) was an East Village hippie who thought it was more important to burn money than draft cards. His wild ideas, devised for their shock value, led to the formation of the Yippie party, which focused on such symbolic protest activities as attempting to levitate the Pentagon. Hoffman wrote several books at the time to publicize his anti-Establishment ideas, among them *Revolution for the Hell of It* (1968) and *Steal This Book* (1971).

5. **(b)** New Left organizations such as SDS differed from the Old Left in several vital ways. Their ideology owed much to the

works of Mao Zedong, Che Guevara, Fidel Castro, and Albert Camus, among others, rather than just those of Marx and Lenin; they believed (at least at first) in "participatory democracy" rather than tightly controlled organization; they considered students to be a major force of change; and, unlike so many veterans of the Old Left's sectarian wars, they didn't condemn Soviet communism. Also, the New Left was a primarily white, middle-class movement rather than one based in the working class.

6. **(b)** In 1969, in response to charges of unfairness in the way draftees were called up, a draft lottery was begun. In the lottery, men received numbers in a random drawing according to date of birth, and those with the lowest numbers were drafted first. Those with numbers higher than a designated cutoff were given 1-H status and not drafted, thus "winning" the lottery.

7. **(a)** The Spring Mobilization to End the War in Vietnam, directed by the Reverend James Bevel, organized huge demonstrations in New York and San Francisco on April 15, 1967. All antiwar groups were invited. In New York, 150 men burned their draft cards, and speakers there included Martin Luther King, Jr., William Sloane Coffin, and Dr. Benjamin Spock.

8. **(b)** In mid-1965, President Lyndon Johnson ordered bombing raids on North Vietnam and increased the number of American troops in South Vietnam. The number of draftees doubled, and in response, nationwide protests, organized by the National Coordinating Committee, took place in sixty cities. On October 16, ten thousand people marched from the Berkeley campus toward the Oakland Army Terminal. When they reached the Oakland city line, however, they were halted by members of the Hell's Angels motorcycle gang, and a violent confrontation ensued. Other marches occurred in New York, Ann Arbor, Philadelphia, and Boston.

9. **(c)** Founded in 1967, the Resistance merged pacifism and action against the war. Its aim was to support those opponents of the war who publicly refused conscription and to help them through the legal proceedings, trials, and sometimes imprisonment that followed.

10. **(a)** Fred Hampton was a member of the Chicago chapter of the Black Panthers. By all accounts an intelligent, much-admired

leader, he was shot dead in his bed during a raid on his apartment by Chicago police on December 4, 1969. The police later charged that Hampton had been shooting at them, but a subsequent inquiry found little evidence to support their claim.

11. **(c)** Founded in 1967, VVAW was a group of veterans who, influenced by the antiwar movement and their own experiences, began to protest the war. In April 1971, in a moving ceremony, more than a thousand VVAW members threw their war medals onto the steps of the U.S. Capitol in Washington. This action demonstrated to many observers that even those who had the most reason to believe in the war had become disillusioned.

12. **(b)** After the U.S. invasion of Cambodia in 1970, campuses across the United States erupted in riots. Kent State in Ohio was no exception, and starting on May 1, confrontations between students and police grew progressively more violent. On May 2, the campus ROTC building was destroyed by fire. By Monday, May 4, the governor had called in the National Guard, and during a face-off between the Guard and students, the order was given to shoot. Four students were killed, and nine others were wounded.

13. **(d)** After 1968, when polls finally began showing that a large percentage of Americans opposed the war, those polls also showed that among those who wanted the war stopped, the reasons most often cited were the belief that the conflict was unwinnable and the cost in American lives was too high. Only a minority were ever concerned about issues of morality, and except at moments like the My Lai massacre, few beyond the organized antiwar activist groups cited the plight of the Vietnamese as a reason for ending American involvement.

14. **(a)** Formed in 1960, Students for a Democratic Society began as an organization of idealist, nonideological, vaguely leftist students who believed in a principle they called "participatory democracy"—that people should be able to have a voice in the political, social, and economic decisions that affect their lives. In the group's early years its members attempted to help the poor through community organizing. Only in the mid-1960s did SDS become involved in the antiwar cause.

15. (d) In September 1964 the administration of the University of California at Berkeley banned leafletting and speechmaking on the Bancroft Strip, an area just off campus. In response, students staged a sit-in and organized the Free Speech Movement, the earliest of the major 1960s campus protest movements.

16. (b) Before the rise of SDS, the NSA, originally founded in 1947, was the most important student organization on many campuses. One of NSA's aims was to bring together students from various countries to discuss international relations. In 1967, *Ramparts* and *The New York Times* revealed that the CIA controlled the NSA's foreign operations, working to keep radicals from attending the international conferences.

17. (a) When SDS broke up in 1969, the Weathermen were one of the factions that emerged from the collapse. Taking their name from a line in a Bob Dylan song, the group rebelled against the inflexible Marxism of the Progressive Labor party and the pacifism of the National Mobilization Committee. Idolizing third-world guerrillas and enamored of "revolutionary" violence, the group believed it was time to "bring the war home!" In October, when the rest of the antiwar movement was occupied with the Moratorium, the Weathermen organized the violent Days of Rage demonstrations in Chicago. Indicted for conspiracy to riot, the group's leadership went underground. For several years thereafter, they frequently placed bombs at sites they considered symbols of U.S. imperialism, including the Pentagon and the U.S. Capitol in Washington, DC.

18. (b) On March 6, 1970, a town house in Greenwich Village exploded. In the ruins were discovered the bodies of three people who had been constructing a bomb. They were identified as Diana Oughton, Terry Robbins, and Ted Gold, all members of the Weathermen. Two other members, Cathy Wilkerson and Kathy Boudin, escaped unhurt and fled underground. Years later Wilkerson gave herself up. Boudin was captured in 1981 following the robbery of a Brink's truck and the murder of two policemen and a guard; she was sentenced to a lengthy prison term.

19. (b) Philip Berrigan, a curate from Baltimore, and Daniel Berrigan, a poet and chaplain at Cornell University, were both arrested as a result of their antiwar activities. Daniel was jailed briefly in 1967 for his role in the March on the Pentagon; Philip was one of the Baltimore Four and spent a summer in prison for pouring blood over draft records. Both brothers were members of the Catonsville Nine and were arrested for destroying draft records with napalm. In 1971, both were tried for conspiracy to kidnap Henry Kissinger and blow up heating systems in federal buildings.

20. **(d)** In October 1969 the Weathermen planned a confrontation with Chicago police, set to occur during the trial of the Chicago Seven. This demonstration was to be part of their campaign to "bring the war home" and turn the streets of America into battlefields like those in Vietnam. Over three hundred people attended the initial rally, then charged through the Chicago streets smashing store windows and overturning cars. Police fought back; six Weathermen were wounded and sixty-eight arrested. A few months later, many Weathermen disappeared to carry on their fight from underground.

21. **(a)** In 1961, soon after Tom Hayden first became involved in student politics at the University of Michigan at Ann Arbor, he was recruited into the tiny campus SDS chapter by Al Haber, the organization's first president. In 1962 Hayden wrote the Port Huron Statement, setting forth the group's political beliefs, and he was elected SDS president. His later political activity included organizing the poor in Newark's ghetto, visiting Hanoi, participating in the 1968 Columbia University protests, and being tried as one of the Chicago Seven.

22. **(d)** On February 4, 1970, students from the University of California at Santa Barbara protested the conviction of the Chicago Seven by rioting in the streets of nearby Isla Vista. At the height of the riot, they burned down the local branch of the Bank of America, chosen as a symbol of capitalism and U.S. imperialism.

23. **(b)** On August 24, 1970, a bomb destroyed Sterling Hall at the University of Wisconsin in Madison. Sterling was the home of the U.S. Army's math research center; the bomb did $6 million in damage and destroyed the life work of five professors and twenty-four graduate students. Postdoctoral student Robert Fussnach was killed in the blast.

24. **(c)** The Stonewall was a gay bar at 53 Christopher Street in Greenwich Village. On June 28, 1969, police raided the bar, and 200 gay patrons fought back. The riot lasted nearly an hour, and subsequent days saw repeated violence on the street outside the bar. This led to a massive rally and protest march that launched a movement for Gay Liberation that was to strengthen throughout the next decade.

25. **(b)** Mark Rudd, a junior at Columbia in 1968, headed a group within the campus SDS chapter called the "action faction" (its rivals were called the "praxis axis"). That spring Rudd was elected chairman of the chapter. Under his leadership, the group demanded that the university withdraw from the Institute for Defense Analysis (an agency that channeled military research contracts to leading universities) and abandon its plan to appropriate a part of Morningside Park, on the edge of Harlem, for a new gymnasium. On April 23, SDS, joined by the Students' Afro-American Society (SAS), staged a rally against the new gym. The demonstration turned into an occupation, first of the main college classroom building and later of three other classroom buildings and the main administration building. The demonstrators set up "communes" in the occupied buildings (SAS by itself held one building); hundreds took part. After six days, New York City police moved in and emptied the buildings by force. After a night of violence, nearly 150 people were injured, and 722 students were arrested. Three weeks later, when Rudd and other demonstration leaders were summoned to face disciplinary charges, a classroom building was again occupied and cleared by police, fires were set, and barricades were built at the gates of the campus. This time 177 people were arrested. Rudd went on to become a national SDS leader and later headed the violent Weathermen faction.

26. **(a)** The U.S. invasion of Cambodia in 1970 led to campus protests across the country. At Jackson State, a largely black college in Jackson, Mississippi, a week of peaceful protest escalated as students began throwing rocks at cars and setting small fires. On May 14, the National Guard was called in. Accompanied by the Jackson police and the highway patrol, the Guard moved to quell a rally in a dormitory. Glass was broken, a shot rang out, and suddenly a barrage of gunfire hit the dorm. Two students in the dorm were killed.

27. **(b)** On May 17, 1968, the Berrigan brothers led a group of Catholics and former Catholics in a raid on the Catonsville, Maryland, draft board. They seized files and burned them with homemade napalm. For this act Daniel Berrigan was sentenced to three years in jail. Both brothers then fled underground, but Daniel was captured by the FBI in August 1970.

28. **(d)** The Youth International party was born out of dissatisfaction with the more serious ideological stances of SDS and the Progressive Labor party. Led by Jerry Rubin and Abbie Hoffman, who met while planning the 1967 March on the Pentagon, the Yippies were responsible for some of the more outrageously theatrical protests of the late 1960s. Among their plans for the Chicago Democratic convention were the nomination of a pig ("Pigasus") for president, the spiking of the city's water supply with LSD, amorous seduction of delegates and their wives, and a protest by naked swimmers in Lake Michigan. Only the first idea was actually carried out. Still, the Yippies were a very visible part of the Chicago protests, and both Hoffman and Rubin were defendants in the trial of the Chicago Seven.

29. **(a)** The Mobe, headed by long-time peace activist David Dellinger, was set up in 1966 to coordinate nationwide antiwar activities. It was the main organizing body behind the 1967 March on the Pentagon and also many of the protests at the 1968 Chicago Democratic convention.

30. **(d)** The Venceremos Brigade was an organization of student volunteers who, starting in late 1969, traveled to Cuba to assist in the sugar cane harvest. Dedicated to helping the cause of third-world anti-imperialism, most returned enthusiastic about what they saw of Cuban socialism; yet a few had difficulty putting aside doubts about the actual nature of the country's Communist regime.

31. **(b)** The Progressive Labor party (PL) was a coalition of Marxist–Leninists and Maoists, ideological hard-liners who were basically Old Left in focus and politics. As SDS began to break apart after 1968, student PL militants began infiltrating it with the goal of taking over the national organization. This was achieved at the June 1969 SDS convention—at the price of a walkout by the Weathermen and other factions, leaving national SDS virtually defunct.

32. **(c)** Bernardine Dohrn was one of the original Weathermen, along with Bill Ayers, Mark Rudd, Jeff Jones, Jim Mellen, and Howie Machtinger. In early 1970, as their activities turned increasingly violent, she and other Weathermen went underground, from whence Dohrn issued various "Communiqués from the Weather Underground."

33. **(c)** The Moratorium of November 15, 1969 (preceded a month earlier by a smaller, similarly named protest), was the largest and politically the most all-inclusive antiwar protest of the 1960s. It involved many thousands of people who had never before publicly protested U.S. involvement in Southeast Asia. A march on Washington had 300,000 participants. Flags were lowered to half-mast all around the country. Schools and universities shut down for periods of teach-ins, concerts, vigils, and marches.

34. **(d)** Surely the most volatile national political convention of our time, the Chicago Democratic convention was displayed to the public in all its gore and fury by television. Before the convention had even begun, there was turmoil: the Yippies vowed to stage a rival convention featuring the pig they had nominated for president, and Mayor Richard Daley, hoping to defuse planned antiwar protests, denied the protesters permission to camp in Lincoln Park. As the convention opened, antiwar Democrats were dismayed by the likelihood that Hubert Humphrey would be nominated; some backed the candidacy of Senator Eugene McCarthy; others sought to draft Ted Kennedy. Racial politics were also evident: the Georgia delegation split between supporters of Governor Lester Maddox and those of Julian Bond, and fistfights broke out on the floor. Black delegates walked out as the nearly all-white Alabama delegation was seated. McCarthy supporters fought with Humphrey supporters. Security guards punched and kicked reporters. Meanwhile, in the streets outside, protestors at first marched behind Ralph Abernathy's Poor People's Campaign, which had a permit to demonstrate. Once the Campaign had gone by, however, police stopped everyone else and told them to turn back. Some protesters sat down in the street and were arrested. Suddenly Daley's police attacked, wielding clubs. Later, TV newscasters broke into the speeches nominating Hubert Humphrey to show violent scenes of what was later called a police riot. In sum, the convention revealed the enormous divisions in the

Democratic party, along with the increasing violence surrounding antiwar protests. It also essentially doomed Hubert Humphrey's campaign. A "peace plank" was proposed but defeated.

35. (c) Bobby Seale was one of the founders of the Black Panther Party. The other three were original members of SDS.

36. (b) Allard K. Lowenstein, formerly of the National Student Association and SNCC, determined in 1967 that the time had come to unite student and liberal antiwar activists around a "Dump Johnson" campaign. Seeking an alternative presidential candidate, he first approached Robert Kennedy, but Kennedy declined. George McGovern was another possibility, but he was running a Senate campaign. So Lowenstein approached Senator Eugene McCarthy of Minnesota, long known for his outspoken opposition to the war. McCarthy finally agreed, and his strong showing in the March 12, 1968, New Hampshire primary proved to Kennedy that Johnson could be beaten. Kennedy then entered the race on March 16, dividing the antiwar activists. On March 31, Johnson announced that he would not seek reelection.

37. (b) Huey Newton, co-founder of the Black Panthers, was convicted in 1967 of killing an Oakland police officer and was sentenced to fifteen years in prison. Many considered the arrest and conviction politically motivated, and "free Huey!" was a routine chant in protest demonstrations. The conviction was later overturned.

38. (a) As originally conceived by David Dellinger and the Mobe, the October 1967 antiwar march was to end at the U.S. Capitol building. However, Jerry Rubin persuaded the organizers to march on the Pentagon instead. A flair for the dramatic made Rubin the logical leader of such an event. The march began with a rally and speeches, then moved across the Potomac toward the Pentagon, led by Norman Mailer and Dr. Benjamin Spock. The National Guard was posted outside the Pentagon, armed and ready. Demonstrators urged the Guardsmen to abandon their posts, and they placed flowers in the barrels of the Guardsmen's guns. Other demonstrators attempted to scale the Pentagon walls and were arrested. Abbie Hoffman led a chanting group that tried symbolically to "levitate" the building. The march was enormous and included dozens of antiwar groups, from the pacifist Mobe people to militant disciples of Che Guevara, who was executed in Bolivia just weeks before.

39. (d) James Reston, Jr., writing in 1970, said that the FBI had received 146,554 draft violation complaints over the previous five years. This was but a percentage of the true number of draft evaders. At that time the apparent number of exiles in Canada was over 50,000 and climbing. Much later, under the Ford adminstration, amnesty was granted to these exiles and to underground or imprisoned draft evaders, as had been traditional in the United States after every war until World War II, when it was granted to only a small minority of protesters.

40. (d) Comedian Dick Gregory, known to civil rights workers for his appearances at protest demonstrations in the South, received wide attention for his part in the events surrounding the 1968 Chicago Democratic convention. Gregory, a native Chicagoan, first addressed protesters at an "unbirthday" party for President Johnson. Later, when marchers were being arrested and beaten, Gregory invited all protesters to march to his home (the police prevented the march from happening). Gregory remains respected for his fasts to promote civil rights and peace.

TEST 4

The Fire Next Time: Civil Rights and Liberation

> The American economy, the American society, the American unconscious are all racist.
>
> —MICHAEL HARRINGTON

1. Ralph Abernathy was associated with
   a. the SCLC
   b. the Albany Movement of 1961
   c. the Montgomery bus boycott of 1957
   d. all of the above

2. What was the Poor People's Campaign?
   a. an effort to bring poor whites and blacks together in protest
   b. the 1968 attempt to nominate Julian Bond for vice-president
   c. an international self-help movement aimed at the third world
   d. a religious revival based on Gandhi's teachings

3. What is the aim of the organization NOW?
   a. ending discrimination against blacks
   b. ending sexual exploitation of children
   c. making pornography illegal
   d. ending discrimination against women

4. The goal of the Mississippi Freedom Summer Project (1964) was
   a. the desegregation of lunch counters
   b. the desegregation of public transportation
   c. voter registration
   d. the overturning of the "separate but equal" decision

5. In what year did the March on Washington led by Martin Luther King, Jr., take place?
   a. 1963
   b. 1965
   c. 1966
   d. 1962

6. In 1965 the Student Nonviolent Coordinating Committee voted to

   a. merge with the NAACP

   b. support the policies of Martin Luther King, Jr.

   c. expel white members from the organization

   d. change its focus from civil rights concerns to antiwar politics

7. A former federal prison off the coast of California made news in 1969 when

   a. American Indians occupied and claimed it

   b. it was reopened to hold 5,000 draft evaders

   c. the National Convention of Women convened there

   d. a huge indoor concert in support of gay rights was held there

8. Ti-Grace Atkinson broke with NOW in the late 1960s and

   a. joined the Black Panthers

   b. ran for Congress on the Socialist ticket

   c. helped organize a radical group called the Feminists

   d. established a publishing house for women writers

9. Which of the these events did *not* happen in Birmingham, Alabama, during April and May 1963?

   a. Nearly 1,000 children were arrested.

   b. Demonstrators were attacked with firehoses and dogs.

   c. President Kennedy sent federal troops to nearby bases.

   d. Jimmie Lee Jackson was killed by state troopers.

10. After John Lewis resigned as president of SNCC in 1966, who replaced him?

   a. E. D. Nixon

   b. Stokely Carmichael

    c. Charles Evers

    d. Hosea Williams

11. The Kerner Commission Report (1968) found that

    a. white racism was the cause of ghetto uprisings

    b. America was splitting into two separate nations

    c. no conspiracy was involved in the 1967 Detroit riots

    d. all of the above

12. What was the original intent of the sit-ins by blacks in the South in the late 1950s?

    a. to integrate public lunch counters

    b. to integrate intercity buses

    c. to integrate Southern public schools

    d. to gain jobs for blacks through affirmative action programs

13. Malcolm X was known for promoting

    a. passive resistance

    b. armed insurrection

    c. black nationalism

    d. universal suffrage

14. The civil rights movement focused on Selma, Alabama, in early 1965 because

    a. Selma was the first truly integrated city in the South

    b. Martin Luther King, Jr., made his home in Selma

    c. the mayor invited the NAACP to make its headquarters there

    d. attempts to register black voters there were met with violence

15. The Civil Rights Act of 1964 attempted to legislate

    a. an end to racial discrimination in public facilities

    b. a ban on poll taxes and discriminatory tests for registering voters

    c. equal protection to all citizens under the law

    d. none of the above

16. What was the "long, hot summer"?

    a. the Watts Riot of 1965

    b. the Mississippi Freedom Summer Project of 1964

    c. a season of riots in American cities in 1967

    d. antiblack violence by Alabama whites in the summer of 1966

17. Gloria Steinem's influence on the women's movement stemmed from her ties to

    a. Hollywood

    b. the Johnson administration

    c. the media

    d. SDS and the antiwar movement

18. Julian Bond, though elected to the Georgia legislature in 1965, was excluded from that body because of his

    a. failure to appear for the opening session

    b. statements condemning the U.S. role in Vietnam

    c. birthdate, which made him too young to sit in the House

    d. public alliance with followers of Malcolm X

19. A doctoral thesis by Kate Millett became a book entitled

    a. *Our Bodies, Ourselves*

    b. *Women and Madness*

    c. *Sexual Politics*

    d. *The Prisoner of Sex*

20. What happened in Memphis, Tennessee, on April 4, 1968?

    a. Malcolm X was shot dead by three Black Muslims.

    b. James Earl Ray killed Martin Luther King, Jr.

c. A black child named Emmett Till was lynched.

d. Governor George Wallace of Alabama was shot.

21. Which of the following is true of civil rights activist Medgar Evers?

    a. He went to jail for refusing to leave a whites-only cafeteria.

    b. He was wounded by police while trying to register voters.

    c. He was murdered by a racist gunman.

    d. He was Ralph Abernathy's chief deputy after the assassination of Martin Luther King, Jr.

22. In what way did Thurgood Marshall reflect the success of the civil rights movement?

    a. He was the first black appointed to the Supreme Court.

    b. He was the first black senator.

    c. He received 10 percent of the vote in the 1968 presidential election.

    d. He served as advisor to President Lyndon Johnson.

23. The 1968 Miss America Pageant in Atlantic City was the scene of

    a. a protest against the exclusion of black women from the competition

    b. one of the first women's liberation demonstrations

    c. a Weathermen bombing

    d. the disqualification of a competitor for singing a civil rights song in the talent competition

24. When was the Equal Rights Amendment passed by Congress?

    a. 1968

    b. 1970

c. 1972

d. It was never passed.

25. What was James Meredith doing when he was shot in 1966?

    a. attempting a lone protest march from Memphis to Jackson

    b. trying to enroll at the University of Mississippi

    c. running for Mississippi state senator

    d. trying to attack Alabama Governor George Wallace

26. Who was awarded the 1964 Nobel Peace Prize?

    a. John F. Kennedy

    b. Martin Luther King, Jr.

    c. Robert F. Kennedy

    d. Ralph Abernathy

27. What was Cesar Chavez's great political achievement?

    a. organizing migrant workers

    b. registering Chicano voters in Los Angeles

    c. being elected senator from California

    d. organizing a Chicano branch of the Weathermen

28. Betty Friedan's 1963 work *The Feminine Mystique* describes

    a. the myth of the happy homemaker

    b. a classless society ruled by women

    c. the breakdown of the family unit

    d. true stories of achievement by women

29. What organization sponsored the 1961 Freedom Rides?

    a. the NAACP

    b. CORE

c. the SCLC

d. SNCC

30. Why was the Mississippi Freedom Democratic party formed in 1964?

   a. to provide an all-black alternative to the all-white regular state Democratic party

   b. to provide an all-white alternative to the newly integrated regular state Democratic party

   c. to provide an integrated alternative to the all-white regular state Democratic party

   d. to elect an alternative black state government

31. Why did prisoners at the New York State prison at Attica revolt in 1971?

   a. Five prisoners were beaten by jail guards.

   b. Food and medical care were inadequate, and political and religious freedoms were restricted.

   c. A black prisoner was murdered by a white prisoner.

   d. Heat and hot water were lacking in their cells.

32. How did Fanny Lou Hamer of the Mississippi Freedom Democratic party help her cause at the 1964 Democratic convention?

   a. She testified on television regarding a beating she had suffered in Mississippi during a drive to register black voters.

   b. She addressed the convention on the subject of black voting rights.

   c. She persuaded Martin Luther King, Jr., to address the convention on her behalf.

   d. She publicly rebuked President Lyndon Johnson for his halfhearted support of the civil rights movement.

33. The Chicano activist conference held in Denver in 1969 called for

    a. equal rights for black and white Hispanics

    b. establishment of a Bureau for Hispanic Affairs and election of Chicano delegates to the 1972 party conventions

    c. aid to Chicano workers and support for anti-imperialist movements in the third world

    d. better day care for Hispanic children

34. When George Wallace became constitutionally ineligible to run again for governor of Alabama, what did he do?

    a. He became more liberal.

    b. He was appointed secretary of the interior.

    c. He ran for state senator.

    d. He had his wife run for governor.

35. What is the central concept of the 1968 book titled *The Female Eunuch?*

    a. the emotional powerlessness of men

    b. the problems of birth control

    c. the symbolic castration of women

    d. the need for liberal abortion laws

36. For what was the organization SCUM best known?

    a. the shooting of Andy Warhol

    b. violent anti-abortion demonstrations

    c. explosions in three Fortune 500 company buildings

    d. violence against voting-rights workers

37. What happened to the civil rights activists Michael Schwerner, James Chaney, and Andrew Goodman in 1964?

    a. They were beaten by angry whites at the end of a Freedom Ride.

b. They were chosen as Mississippi Freedom Democratic party delegates to the Democratic national convention.

c. They were honored by President Lyndon Johnson for their work in voter registration drives.

d. They were murdered by white racists in Mississippi.

38. Which black activist approved of riots as "a dress rehearsal for revolution"?

a. Stokely Carmichael

b. H. Rap Brown

c. Malcolm X

d. Huey Newton

39. What were the greatest triumphs of NAACP leader Roy Wilkins?

a. the school integration ruling of 1955 and the Civil Rights Act of 1964

b. his election for two terms as the first black senator from Alabama

c. the organization of militant black separatist movements in New York and San Francisco

d. his nomination for vice-president in 1968 and for president in 1972

40. What incident set off the Watts riot of 1965 in Los Angeles?

a. the rape of a black girl by a white gang

b. the murder of a black robbery suspect by white police

c. the arrest of a black man for drunk driving

d. the death of Martin Luther King, Jr.

TEST 4: *Explanatory Answers*

1. **(d)** Ralph Abernathy was the young minister of the First Baptist Church in Montgomery, Alabama, when he became involved in organizing the 1957 boycott of the city's buses. When Martin Luther King, Jr., founded the SCLC, Abernathy was one of the first members. After King's death in 1968, he headed the organization for ten years. Among the actions King and Abernathy helped organize was the 1961 Albany Movement, an effort to desegregate that Georgia town.

2. **(a)** In 1968, Martin Luther King, Jr., was looking for a way to expand his political base. He planned a march on Washington that would bring together poor people from all parts of the country in protest against the American economic system that kept them in thrall. Before the plan could be realized, King was assassinated; but Ralph Abernathy led the march, which took place from May 13 to June 24. The event culminated in a tent-in on the Washington Mall. The Poor People's Campaign went on to stage a march at the Chicago Democratic convention.

3. **(d)** The National Organization for Women (NOW) was established in 1966. Its founder was Betty Friedan, and its aim is equality for women in all areas of life.

4. **(c)** The Mississippi Freedom Summer Project was organized in 1964 by an umbrella group of civil rights groups called the Council of Federated Organizations. In the Project, CORE, SNCC, and student volunteers from across the country worked to register black voters in Mississippi. The Project was marked by violence: three volunteers were murdered, dozens were injured, and hundreds were arrested. Students from the Project who returned to school that fall brought their new-found activism to the antiwar movement.

5. **(a)** On August 28, 1963, nearly a quarter of a million demonstrators marched on Washington, DC, to protest the violations of blacks' civil rights. The march culminated in the famous "I Have a Dream" speech by Martin Luther King, Jr., delivered from the steps of the Lincoln Memorial. At the time

it was the largest such gathering ever held in the nation's capital.

6. **(c)** The Student Nonviolent Coordinating Committee (SNCC) was founded in 1960 on the campus of Shaw University in Raleigh, North Carolina. Its intended goal was to organize the various student groups conducting sit-ins throughout the South. SNCC workers, white and black, strove to enter and join a community, live with the people there, and work directly toward desegregation. After the violent Selma campaign of 1965, however, SNCC's black members, no longer willing to meet violence with passive resistance, broke with Martin Luther King, Jr.'s SCLC and became increasingly militant and separatist. When SNCC's white volunteers were expelled in 1965, many returned to the North, where they applied what they had learned to the antiwar movement or to social reform.

7. **(a)** The militant American Indian Movement (AIM) was founded in 1968 by Dennis Banks and Clyde Bellancourt. On November 20, 1969, eighty-nine members of the organization took over Alcatraz, a former prison in San Francisco Bay. They held the island for nineteen months, demanding its return to the Indians and money to establish a center for Indian culture. Negotiations with the government continued until federal marshals moved in and removed the last fifteen protesters in 1971. AIM went on to sponsor a short-lived occupation of the Bureau of Indian Affairs in 1972 and a 69-day takeover of Wounded Knee, South Dakota, in 1973, during which they demanded a review of existing treaties between the United States and the Indian tribes.

8. **(c)** Ti-Grace Atkinson was president of the New York chapter of NOW in 1968 when she broke with the organization over its hierarchical structure. The New York chapter was already far more radical than most, and many members disagreed with the national organization on details of issues such as abortion and women's liberation. Atkinson and her followers established the October 17th Movement, renamed the Feminists in 1969. Their actions included supporting abortionists and issuing dozens of papers on feminism, marriage, and the role of women in society. Atkinson later left the group in a dispute over a resolution requiring group consensus for any

contact with the media (despite the Feminists' initial plan to work as a group of equals, Atkinson had always been spokesperson).

9. **(d)** Twenty-six-year-old Jimmie Lee Jackson was shot and killed by state troopers during a demonstration in Selma, Alabama, in February 1965. In Birmingham in April 1963, Martin Luther King, Jr., launched a desegregation campaign (called Project "C" for "Confrontation"). Birmingham, Alabama's largest city, was already infamous for its mob attack on Freedom Riders in 1961. As it had been in 1961, power in the city was in the hands of the commissioner of public safety, Eugene "Bull" Connor. The initial demonstrations were put down with great violence. In the first three weeks of protests, hundreds were jailed, among them King and Ralph Abernathy. From jail King wrote a famous letter to his fellow clergymen clearly articulating his reasons for direct action. With his release, the demonstration leaders decided to send black children into the streets. On May 2, thousands of children marched toward downtown Birmingham and were arrested in droves. The next day more children marched, but Connor turned police dogs and firehoses on the demonstrators. Immediately the black community, which had been split over the tactics of the SCLC, rallied around the cause. By May 6, thousands were in jail, television and newspapers were showing daily attacks on children, and the Kennedy administration was forced to intervene. Negotiators were sent from Washington, and a desegregation plan was worked out with local business owners. However, the Ku Klux Klan and Connor urged whites to ignore the accord, and the motel where King was staying was firebombed, as was the home of his brother. Finally Kennedy dispatched federal troops to nearby Fort McClellan in hopes that their presence would deter further violence, and his ploy worked.

10. **(b)** John Lewis, objecting to SNCC's militant turn, resigned as president in 1966 and was replaced by Stokely Carmichael. The following year Carmichael left to join the Black Panthers and ceded his post to H. Rap Brown. Carmichael later became involved in politics in Africa and joined a movement in Guinea to overthrow its military dictatorship. Of the others listed, E. D. Nixon, active in the Brotherhood of Sleeping Car Porters, helped organize the Montgomery bus boycott. Charles Evers

took over his brother Medgar's position in the NAACP after Medgar Evers was killed. Hosea Williams was affiliated with the SCLC.

11. **(d)** After the riots in the ghettos of Detroit and Newark during the summer of 1967, President Lyndon Johnson set up the National Advisory Commission on Civil Disorders to investigate the violence. This commission was chaired by Governor Otto Kerner of Illinois. The commission report, released on February 29, 1968, blamed the riots on white racism and found no evidence of conspiracy. The report said that America was dividing into two separate nations, one black and one white. It found that even the advances of the civil rights movement had not brought blacks out of the ghettos, and it called for reforms in housing, jobs, welfare, and education. Some radicals thought the report did not go far enough in identifying the racist causes of black poverty; it did, however, signal a change in focus from political reform to economic reform.

12. **(a)** James Lawson, a former student at the divinity school of Vanderbilt University in Nashville, Tennessee, was southern field secretary of an organization called the Fellowship of Reconciliation. He based himself in Nashville and traveled throughout the South running workshops on nonviolence. Diane Nash of Vanderbilt was one of his pupils, and she and John Lewis founded the Nashville Student Movement. In the late 1950s this group began a campaign to desegregate the lunch counters of Nashville department stores. Soon afterward, in February 1960, a sit-in by four black college students at an F. W. Woolworth store in Greensboro, North Carolina, gained national attention. The Nashville group joined the Greensboro students by sitting in at branches of the same stores in Nashville. They were soon copied by students in Alabama and Florida, and the sit-ins led to boycotts. The Nashville students staged sit-ins through the spring of 1960, and in May six Nashville lunch counters began serving black patrons.

13. **(c)** Born Malcolm Little, Malcolm X (1925–1965) became a Black Muslim, or follower of Elijah Muhammad, while serving time in prison for burglary. After his release, he became a minister famous for his oratory and for his support of black separatism. In 1963 he broke with Elijah Muhammad and converted to orthodox Islam. His followers, the Organization of Afro-American Unity, supported black power but not black

supremacy; the possibility of reconciliation between the races was left open. Malcolm's charisma and power base were a threat to the Black Muslims, and in 1965 he was assassinated by members of that group while speaking at the Audubon Ballroom in New York City.

14. **(d)** SNCC workers in Selma had met increased resistance from white deputies of Sheriff James Clark as they tried to integrate lunch counters and register voters in the town. In January 1965, Martin Luther King, Jr., and the SCLC began a campaign of protest marches and registration activities designed to provoke the sheriff and his men into demonstrating their brutal methods for television cameras and reporters. The strategy worked; King had just been awarded the Nobel Peace Prize, and the sight of him and his followers, many of them children, being beaten and hauled off to jail awakened Northerners to the violence facing protesters in the South.

15. **(a)** The 1964 Civil Rights Act was enacted to bar discrimination on the grounds of race or religion and to provide for the integration of public facilities. The law made it possible for the federal government to sue or withhold funds when discrimination was found to exist. The other laws described are the Voting Rights Act of 1965 and the Fourteenth Amendment (1868). Discrimination in housing was the theme of the 1968 Civil Rights Act.

16. **(c)** By 1967, the nonviolent civil rights movement was losing its appeal; black power was gaining followers. The difference between the two was one of approach to social change, and the speed advocated by the black power movement was especially attractive to those who had yet to achieve anything from the civil rights advances: people at the bottom of the socioeconomic ladder. There is still debate over how spontaneous or unified in purpose the riots of 1967 were, but certainly they cannot be separated from a growing militancy and desire for action. Ghetto uprisings in Detroit and Newark were particularly devastating, leaving over sixty dead and thousands more injured or homeless.

17. **(c)** Steinem gained some measure of fame with an article published in 1963 in *Show* magazine entitled "I Was a Playboy Bunny." She detailed the exploitation of ill-paid waitresses at the world-famous Playboy Club, but although the article won

the interest of some feminists, Steinem herself came late to the cause. She wrote for *Esquire*, *Ladies' Home Journal*, and other magazines before landing a column in Clay Felker's *New York*. Here she was finally able to talk about politics, and her writing and lecturing made her widely known as a symbol of the women's movement. With the founding and success of *Ms.* magazine, Steinem proved once and for all that there was a wide audience for feminist writing.

18. **(b)** Bond had been SNCC's director of communications and had participated in sit-ins in the early 1960s. In 1965 he won a seat in the Georgia state legislature, but that body refused to seat him because he had publicly called America's involvement in Vietnam a violation of international law. Even though the voters reelected him twice, Bond was not allowed to take his seat until 1966, when the Supreme Court declared his exclusion unconstitutional. He went on to split the Georgia delegation during the 1968 Democratic convention, and he became the first black to be nominated for the vice-presidency, an honor he had to decline because he was too young for the post.

19. **(c)** Kate Millett's book was published in 1970 and set off a media storm. Millett, education director of the New York chapter of NOW and an artist by trade, was canonized by *Time* as the ideologue of the women's liberation movement. Immediately she became the most popular movement speaker on the lecture circuit—until her announcement of her bisexuality scandalized the same media that had formerly acclaimed her. The authors of the other books listed are the Boston Women's Health Collective, Phyllis Chesler, and Norman Mailer.

20. **(b)** Martin Luther King, Jr., (1929–1968) was in the middle of organizing a Memphis garbagemen's strike when he was assassinated by James Earl Ray—probably a hired killer. His final speech, delivered the day before, contained these words: "I've seen the promised land. I may not get there with you. But I want you to know tonight that we, as a people, will get to the promised land. And so I'm happy tonight. I'm not worried about anything. I'm not fearing any man. Mine eyes have seen the glory of the coming of the Lord." The assassination led to riots in cities across the nation.

21. **(c)** Medgar Evers (1925–1963) served as the NAACP's Mississippi field director after his rejection from law school in 1954.

In 1963 the civil rights campaign against segregation in Jackson became heated; many segregationists believed that if Evers were eliminated, the furor would stop. On June 12, Evers was murdered outside his home in the sight of his family. His alleged killer was tried twice for the murder, but the trials resulted in hung juries. Evers was buried in Arlington National Cemetery.

22. **(a)** Thurgood Marshall was a lawyer for the NAACP, arguing and winning the landmark 1955 Supreme Court case *Brown v. Board of Education.* He was appointed circuit court judge by President Kennedy, and in 1965 President Johnson appointed him solicitor general. In 1967 Marshall was confirmed as a Supreme Court justice, the first and so far the only black to sit on the Supreme Court.

23. **(b)** On September 7, 1968, two hundred women from the Women's Liberation Front gathered outside the convention hall in Atlantic City and threw girdles, brassieres, false eyelashes, and high heels into a "freedom trash can," symbolizing their liberation from the uncomfortable accoutrements of beauty. They then crowned a sheep as Miss America. This was one of the first organized protests of the women's liberation movement.

24. **(c)** In 1972, Congress passed the Equal Rights Amendment, which forbade discrimination on the grounds of sex. However, to become law, the amendment had to be ratified by thirty-eight state legislatures within ten years, and this was never achieved.

25. **(a)** In 1962, James Meredith became the first black student to enter the University of Mississippi; his enrollment caused riots and violence. After graduation he continued his activism; in 1966, to promote voter registration, he attempted a lone protest march from Memphis, Tennessee, to Jackson, Mississippi. Ten miles inside the Mississippi border, he was shot and wounded by a white man; Martin Luther King, Jr., and Stokely Carmichael completed the march.

26. **(b)** After the 1963 March on Washington, Martin Luther King, Jr., was awarded the Nobel Peace Prize in recognition of his nonviolent methods and his work for black civil rights. The Nobel Prize winner is decided by a committee of the Norwegian parliament, and winners are given a gold medal and a large cash award.

27. **(a)** Born in Arizona in 1929, Cesar Chavez worked as a migrant field hand in California before he began organizing grape pickers into the National Farm Workers Association in 1962. He led boycotts against growers who treated workers unfairly, and in 1972 his organization, now known as the United Farm Workers, became a member union of the AFL-CIO.

28. **(a)** Following the women's suffragist campaigns in the early part of the century and the influx of women into industry during World War II, Americans in the postwar period were once again content to believe that women were meant only to bear children and manage the home. Betty Friedan's controversial 1963 book directly challenged this idea. The book was enormously influential in spelling out the issues that would be the foundation of the new women's movement, especially the need to alter society's perception of "appropriate" roles. Friedan went on to become the first president of NOW in 1966.

29. **(b)** The Congress of Racial Equality (CORE), a civil rights organization founded in the 1940s, decided in 1961 to stage a Freedom Ride, an attempt by black and white activists to integrate Southern intercity buses and bus depots. CORE leaders hoped the Ride would create a crisis and focus attention on blacks' lack of civil rights. The riders rode two public bus lines and, at each stopping point, entered segregated restaurants and waiting rooms. In South Carolina and Alabama they were attacked and badly beaten. However, President Kennedy ordered protection by federal marshals, and the Ride continued. By the time the riders reached Mississippi, most of them had been arrested for violating Jim Crow laws. The Ride spawned dozens of other Freedom Rides and focused national attention on the plight of blacks in the South.

30. **(c)** Organized in 1964 by Bob Moses and Jim Forman of SNCC, the Mississippi Freedom Democratic party (MFDP) was to be an integrated alternative to the all-white regular state Democratic party; the idea was to challenge the regulars for Mississippi's seats at the 1964 national Democratic convention. Obeying Democratic party rules precisely, members elected an integrated delegation. However, when this group arrived at the convention in Atlantic City, it was refused seating; the

Johnson administration was fearful of alienating traditional Southern Democrats. Eventually a compromise was reached whereby even though the MFDP was excluded in 1964, the Democratic party committed itself to the integration of state delegations in the future.

31. **(b)** On September 9, 1971, 1,200 inmates of Attica State Prison revolted, taking 38 guards hostage. Their demands were for better food and medical care and increased political and religious freedom. After several days the prison was stormed and recaptured by over 1,000 state troopers; 9 hostages and 29 prisoners were killed.

32. **(a)** Fanny Lou Hamer was vice-chairman of the Mississippi Freedom Democratic party in 1964, when she headed the delegation that challenged all-white party regulars for Mississippi's seats at the Democratic national convention. At first refused entry to the convention floor, she gave a moving interview on national television in which she declared that she had not "come all this way just to have no place to sit down." She also described the beatings she had suffered in Mississippi because of her voter registration efforts. The sympathy she evoked forced Democratic leaders to guarantee that in the future no more all-white delegations would be admitted.

33. **(c)** By 1960, Chicanos were the second-largest minority in the United States. Chicano youth organizations were formed, and in 1969 activists met in Denver to prepare a list of movement aims. The goals they defined were several: community control of Hispanic neighborhoods, equality of Spanish with English, support for foreign movements against U.S. imperialism, and help for Hispanic workers in the United States. The members refused to admit blacks to the conference, causing a walkout by the delegation from Puerto Rico. In the end, few lasting changes resulted from the conference.

34. **(d)** In 1966, George Wallace's wife Lurleen ran for governor of Alabama because her husband was constitutionally ineligible for reelection. She won and was governor until her death in 1968. Wallace in the meantime staged an independent run for the presidency and received 14 percent of the vote.

35. **(c)** Written in 1968, *The Female Eunuch* by Germaine Greer explores the methods by which women have been dominated and psychologically deformed by men. In matters of intellect and sexuality, men, says Greer, have used psychological techniques to "castrate" women, leaving them powerless and, worse, willing to do the same to their daughters in order to prevent *their* sufferings at the hands of men. The book became a classic of feminist literature.

36. **(a)** In June 1968, Valerie Solanis, an actress who had appeared in one of Andy Warhol's films, shot and wounded the artist-director. She later explained that she wanted him to pay attention to her, and she wrote as a justification the SCUM (Society for Cutting Up Men) Manifesto, a violent diatribe against the male sex.

37. **(d)** As volunteers in the Mississippi Freedom Summer Project, Schwerner, Chaney, and Goodman traveled together to Philadelphia, Mississippi, in June 1964 to help register voters. Schwerner and Goodman were whites from the North; Chaney was a local black activist. Outside of town the three were arrested for speeding by the local sheriff. They were fined and released but were never seen alive again. The FBI joined in the search, and two months later the young men's bodies were found. All three had been shot. Twenty-one whites were arrested in connection with the murders, but only one, a deputy sheriff, served any time in jail. The murders were most likely ordered by the Ku Klux Klan.

38. **(b)** H. Rap Brown took over the chair of SNCC from Stokely Carmichael in 1967. His philosophy was much more radical and violent than Carmichael's, and he openly supported the idea of guerrilla warfare against white oppression.

39. **(a)** Roy Wilkins (1901–1981) was the leader of the National Association for the Advancement of Colored People from 1931 to 1977. During the 1950s and 1960s he continually sought racial integration through nonviolent means such as legislation and court orders; the 1955 school integration ruling and the 1964 Civil Rights Act owed much to his efforts. In the late 1960s his nonviolent stance was often criticized by more militant blacks.

40. **(c)** In Watts, Los Angeles' black ghetto, conditions had been tense for a long time before 1965. Caught between gang warfare and the white police force, the inhabitants were frustrated, and their frustration grew when they heard of civil rights victories in the South. On August 11, a black man was stopped in the middle of the neighborhood and arrested for drunk driving, and with a cry of "Burn, baby, burn!" onlookers became violent. During the following week, at least thirty thousand blacks took part in the riot, looting stores and destroying property. Finally, the National Guard was called in, and by August 18 the riot was over, leaving more than twenty dead.

TEST 5

Magical Mystery Tour: Geography

> The old civic, state, and national groupings have become unworkable.
>
> —MARSHALL McLUHAN

1. In which of the following countries did the United States intervene militarily in the 1960s?

   a. the Dominican Republic

   b. Israel

   c. Iran

   d. all of the above

2. Why was the Vietnamese port of Da Nang important to Americans?

   a. It was the site of an important U.S. military base.

   b. It was where captured American GIs were paraded before crowds of hostile North Vietnamese.

   c. It was where the president of South Vietnam was assassinated in 1963.

   d. It was the site of the first U.S. military casualty in Vietnam in 1955.

3. Which of the following countries were members of SEATO?

   a. North Vietnam, China, and the Soviet Union

   b. India, Burma, Spain, Portugal, the United States, and the Philippines

   c. the United States, France, Great Britain, New Zealand, Australia, Pakistan, Thailand, and the Philippines

   d. Laos, Cambodia, South Vietnam, and the United States

Questions 4–9 are based on the following map.

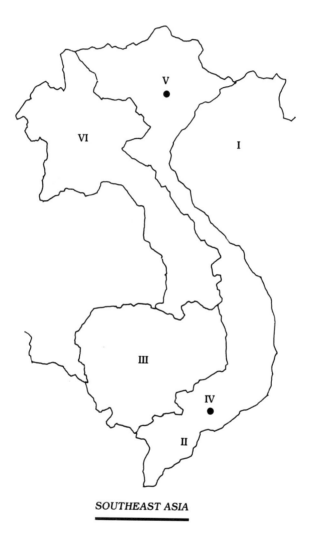

SOUTHEAST ASIA

4. Which labeled area is the Mekong Delta?

  a. I **b.** V **c.** II **d.** IV

5. Which labeled area is the Gulf of Tonkin?

  a. VI **b.** IV **c.** III **d.** I

6. Which labeled location is Saigon?

  a. II **b.** IV **c.** V **d.** III

7. Which labeled location is Hanoi?

  a. I **b.** IV **c.** V **d.** VI

8. Which labeled area is Cambodia?

  a. III **b.** V **c.** I **d.** II

9. Which labeled area is Laos?

  a. I **b.** VI **c.** IV **d.** III

.

Questions 10–13 are based on the following map.

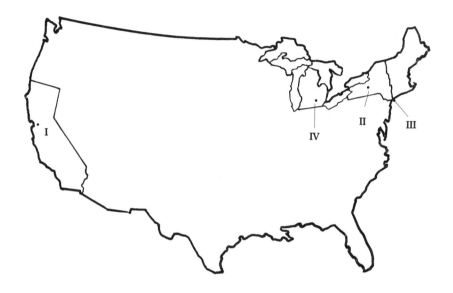

10. What happened in 1964 at the university labeled I?

  a. Four students were shot dead by National Guard troops.

  b. Students met to plan a national campaign against the draft.

  c. Students staged sit-ins and strikes for freedom of speech.

  d. Students broke into the local draft board and destroyed records.

11. What happened in 1969 at the university labeled II?

  a. SDS members blew up a chemistry lab, blinding a custodian.

  b. Students issued a manifesto calling for abandonment of the traditional curriculum.

c. Students staged a sit-in at the ROTC building.

d. Armed black students occupied the student union building.

12. What happened at the university labeled III in 1968?

a. Students gathered outside the president's office to burn their draft cards.

b. Demonstrators disrupted a speech by Hubert Humphrey.

c. Students occupied administration and classroom buildings to protest the building of a gymnasium.

d. Students boycotted classes to protest the presence of Dow Chemical Company recruiters.

13. What happened at the university labeled IV in 1965?

a. Professors and students participated in teach-ins exploring the reasons behind American intervention in Vietnam.

b. A student immolated himself to protest the war in Vietnam.

c. SDS led protests against CIA recruitment.

d. The May 2 Movement opened a Free University on campus.

14. Which of the following African countries achieved independence from France in the 1960s?

a. Angola and Mozambique

b. Mali and Senegal

c. Rhodesia and Kenya

d. Somalia and Ethiopia

Questions 15–18 are based on the following map.

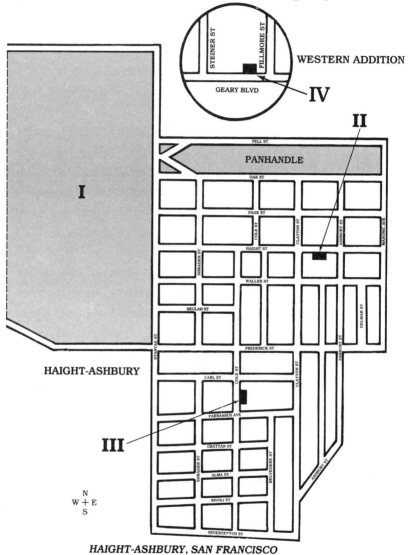

WESTERN ADDITION

PANHANDLE

HAIGHT-ASHBURY

HAIGHT-ASHBURY, SAN FRANCISCO

I. Golden Gate Park
II. The Psychedelic Shop
III. Digger Storefront
IV. The Fillmore (*Western Addition*)

15. What pioneering event took place at location I?

   a. the first Be-In

   b. the first march protesting U.S. involvement in Vietnam

   c. the first Acid Test

   d. the first Grateful Dead concert

16. What kind of enterprise flourished at location II?

   a. an art store where op art posters and paintings were sold

   b. a store that sold products of interest to LSD users

   c. a café where diners played music and recited poetry

   d. a discotheque where new bands got their start

17. What kind of items were given away at location III?

   a. drugs

   b. concert tickets

   c. food and medical care

   d. books and pamphlets

18. What was offered at location IV?

   a. free lodging for newly arrived hippies

   b. free health services for street people

   c. weekly rock dances

   d. free copies of underground newspapers

19. What important event occurred at the town of Khe Sanh in Vietnam?

   a. the last battle of the Vietnam War

   b. the murder of an American nurse by Viet Cong soldiers

   c. the encirclement and siege of American troops by Viet Cong forces

   d. the first use of napalm in the Vietnam War

20. Which of these African countries achieved independence from Belgium in the 1960s?

   a. Botswana and Zambia

   b. Chad and the Sudan

   c. Togo and Benin

   d. Rwanda and Zaire

21. Besides the United States, which other nations sent troops to support South Vietnam?

   a. Australia, Canada, and France

   b. Australia, New Zealand, the Philippines, Thailand, and South Korea

   c. Burma, Laos, North Korea, Thailand, and South Korea

   d. Indonesia, Japan, and the Philippines

22. Which was the only state to vote for George McGovern in 1972?

    a. Minnesota

    b. California

    c. Massachusetts

    d. Maine

23. What was the nearest town to the site of the 1969 Woodstock Music and Arts Fair?

    a. Woodstock, Vermont

    b. Woodstock, New York

    c. Bethel, New York

    d. Monterey, California

24. The Geneva accords of 1954 established a demilitarized zone that

    a. divided Vietnam along the 17th parallel

    b. created a border between Cambodia and Vietnam

    c. separated North Vietnam and South Vietnam at the Mekong River

    d. later became known as the Iron Triangle

Questions 25–28 are based on the following map.

FOUR SOUTHERN STATES

25. The route of the 1965 March from Selma to Montgomery
is represented by the

  a. dotted line

  b. dashed line

  c. solid line

  d. none of the above

26. Part of the route of an early Freedom Ride is represented
by the

  a. dotted line

  b. dashed line

  c. solid line

  d. none of the above

27. "Ole Miss" is in the city on the map labeled

  a. I **b.** II **c.** III **d.** IV

28. Birmingham is the city on the map labeled

    a. I   **b.** II   **c.** III   **d.** IV

29. In which country did the CIA establish a "secret army"?

    a. North Vietnam

    b. Chile

    c. Cuba

    d. Laos

30. The city once called Saigon is now called

    a. Hanoi

    b. Kampuchea

    c. Ho Chi Minh City

    d. Dien Bien Phu

31. Which Caribbean islands gained independence in the 1960s?

    a. Bahamas, Guadeloupe, and Martinique

    b. the Cayman Islands and Puerto Rico

    c. Barbuda, Curaçao, the Dominican Republic, and Haiti

    d. Barbados, Jamaica, and Trinidad and Tobago

32. Where was "Resurrection City"?

    a. on the Mall in Washington, DC

    b. at the starting point of the March to Montgomery

    c. five miles outside Atlanta, Georgia

    d. on the campus of the University of Mississippi

Questions 33–37 are based on the following map.

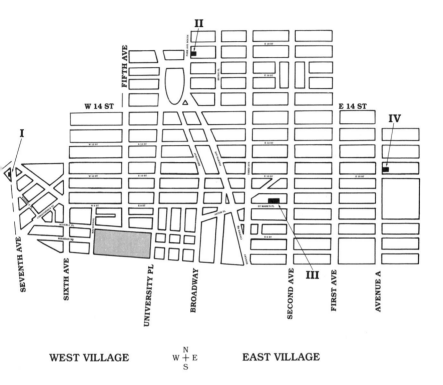

SECTION OF GREENWICH VILLAGE, NEW YORK CITY

I. The Village Vanguard
II. Max's Kansas City
III. The Dom-Electric Circus
IV. The Psychedelicatessan

33. A club that opened in 1966 and attracted artists and rock musicians is the place on the map labeled

a. I **b.** II **c.** III **d.** IV

34. An exhibition by Andy Warhol became the place on the map labeled

a. I **b.** II **c.** III **d.** IV

35. To hear Lenny Bruce in the late 1950s or Miles Davis in the late 1960s, you might have gone to the place on the map labeled

a. I **b.** II **c.** III **d.** IV

36. The first head shop in New York was the place on the map labeled

a. I **b.** II **c.** III **d.** IV

37. The shaded area of the map represents

a. Tompkins Square Park

b. Union Square

c. Washington Square Park

d. Columbia University

38. Which of the following is *not* a Vietnamese province?

a. Vientiane

b. Quang Tri

c. Binh Dinh

d. Pleiku

39. What do these names have in common: Bragg, Pendleton, Lejeune?

a. They are all locations of university campuses.

b. They are all names of military training centers.

c. They were all code names for sites in Cambodia.

d. They were all sites of riots during the "long, hot summer."

40. Which African countries gained independence from Great Britain in the 1960s?

a. Kenya, Nigeria, and Uganda

b. Rhodesia, Sierra Leone, and Tanzania

c. Gambia, Lesotho, and Malawi

d. all of the above

TEST 5: Explanatory Answers

1. **(a)** When Rafael Trujillo, dictator of the Dominican Republic, was assassinated in 1961, the moderate leftist Juan Bosch Gavino was elected president. However, in 1963 his regime was overthrown by rightists, and civil war broke out. President Lyndon Johnson, claiming that Communists controlled the pro-Bosch forces, sent U.S. troops to occupy the capital. Following a new election, an authoritarian regime headed by Joaquin Balaguer took power.

2. **(a)** During the Vietnam War, Da Nang was the site of an enormous U.S. military base. Many of the war's massive bombing raids were launched from Da Nang. Starting as early as April 1965, the base was attacked repeatedly by enemy forces. Following the evacuation of American forces, it fell to North Vietnamese troops on March 30, 1975.

3. **(c)** SEATO, the Southeast Asia Treaty Organization, was an alliance formed in 1954 after the French defeat and withdrawal from Indochina. Its purpose was to prevent further Communist gains throughout southern Asia and the southwestern Pacific. Its effectiveness was limited, however, because two key countries, India and Burma, refused membership. After the Communist victories in Indochina in 1975, SEATO was disbanded in 1977.

4. **(c)** The Mekong Delta region, located at the mouth of the Mekong River, is a series of marshes and small rivers where rice is grown. During the early years of the Vietnam War, the area was held by the Viet Cong; their guerrilla tactics were well suited to the swampy terrain. In 1967 a special force called the Riverine was formed by the United States to clear the Mekong, and by July of that year the Riverine had pushed the Viet Cong westward.

5. **(d)** In the summer of 1964, the American destroyer U.S.S. *Maddox* sailed into the Gulf of Tonkin on patrol. After apparently being fired upon by a North Vietnamese vessel, it was joined by two other destroyers. On July 31, torpedoes were allegedly sighted on the ships' radar, and the destroyers opened fire. On August 5, American planes bombed North Vietnamese bases. At that point Congress, eager to back the show of force (and urged by the Johnson administration), voted to approve

the so-called Tonkin Gulf Resolution, which allowed the president to send forces into Vietnam without a declaration of war.

6. **(b)** Saigon was the capital of South Vietnam until its fall to North Vietnamese troops on April 30, 1975. During the Vietnam War it was the headquarters for U.S. forces in the country and the site of the U.S. embassy. In January 1968, during the Tet offensive, the embassy was briefly attacked by the Viet Cong. After the city was conquered in 1975, it was renamed to honor the former North Vietnamese leader.

7. **(c)** Hanoi was the center of fighting between the French and the Viet Minh during the 1940s and 1950s. After Vietnam was divided in 1954, it became the capital of North Vietnam; in the late 1960s and early 1970s it was subjected to heavy American bombing. Following the fall of Saigon in 1975, it became the capital of the reunified Socialist Republic of Vietnam.

8. **(a)** Cambodia achieved independence from France in 1953. During the Vietnam War it attempted to remain neutral; nevertheless, the North Vietnamese used it as a supply route, and the Americans subjected it to heavy bombing. In 1970, following a coup in Cambodia that installed a pro-American regime, American and South Vietnamese forces entered the country in pursuit of the North Vietnamese. The Americans later withdrew, but a fierce civil war followed between the new government and Cambodian Communist guerrillas called the Khmer Rouge. The regime, despite massive American aid, could not survive, and in 1975, the guerrillas captured the capital, Phnom Penh. They proceeded to force much of the population into rural labor camps, where huge numbers were murdered and many more died of starvation. In 1978 Vietnamese troops invaded the country, and a new government, friendly to Vietnam, was established.

9. **(b)** Laos borders both northern and southern Vietnam. Like Cambodia, during the Vietnam War it was used as a supply route by the North Vietnamese and subjected to heavy American bombing. After the victories of the Communist forces in Vietnam and Cambodia in 1975, Laos came under the full control of the pro-Vietnamese Laotian Communists in a gradual and relatively peaceful transfer of power.

10. **(c)** Berkeley students in 1964 were fervent supporters of the civil rights movement, and many speeches and demonstrations were held on what was called the Bancroft Strip, an area just off campus. On September 14, the dean of students forbade speechmaking there, infuriating many students. During the fall semester sit-ins were held, and a strike in November and December, supported by faculty, closed classes until just before Christmas.

11. **(d)** In 1969 black students at Cornell University demanded the establishment of an Afro-American Center. The university, however, did not respond; and when a cross was burned on campus that April, the black students occupied Willard Straight Hall. When white students tried to force their way in, some of the black students armed themselves. The university president promised not to take action against the militants, and $240,000 was provided to establish the Center.

12. **(c)** In the spring of 1968, Columbia University unveiled plans to appropriate a part of Morningside Park, located in Harlem, as the site for a new gymnasium. Students accused the university of racism and, in protest, took over Hamilton Hall on April 23. Soon four more buildings, including Low Library, were also occupied, and the demonstrators, who now numbered in the hundreds, were also demanding that the university sever its ties with the Institute for Defense Analysis, an agency that channeled defense contracts to university research labs. After nearly a week, New York City police cleared the buildings; many demonstrators were injured, and more than 700 were arrested.

13. **(a)** In March 1965, forty-nine professors at the University of Michigan at Ann Arbor suggested that a day be set aside for university-wide discussions of the war in Vietnam. The March 24 session, which involved nearly 4,000 students and teachers, lasted all night and spawned similar teach-ins at Columbia, NYU, Rutgers, and the University of Oregon.

14. **(b)** After World War II, France's empire in Africa included Mali, Senegal, the Ivory Coast, Guinea, Algeria, Morocco, Tunisia, the French Cameroons, and French Equatorial Africa. In 1954 an armed rebellion broke out in Algeria, and years of fighting followed. In the late 1950s France, under a new government headed by Charles de Gaulle, offered its African colonies the

choice of self-government within a French-led community or complete independence. Guinea chose complete independence, and Senegal, Mali, the Ivory Coast, the Cameroons (now Cameroon), and French Equatorial Africa (now the Central African Republic, the People's Republic of the Congo, and Chad) followed in 1960 (Morocco and Tunisia had both achieved independence in 1956). Algeria finally became independent in 1962 after the end of the Algerian War.

15. **(a)** In January 1967 the Diggers and hippies of the Haight organized what they called "the First Human Be-In" in Golden Gate Park, an event that was advertised as "a union of love and activism." The Be-In featured gurus, the Merry Pranksters, and rock bands, and thousands of people attended.

16. **(b)** The Psychedelic Shop on Haight Street opened in 1966 to sell items such as psychedelic literature, incense, marijuana paraphernalia, paisley clothing, and tickets for concerts. The owner later placed theater seats in the window so that people could watch the ever-changing drama of Haight Street.

17. **(c)** In 1966 the Diggers, a band of countercultural anarchists, began giving away free stew and fruit each day in Golden Gate Park, acting on their philosophy that all things belonged to everyone. Later they opened this storefront to provide free clothing and a free doctor (though this latter was hardly sufficient to treat the drug-related medical problems that soon engulfed the Haight). The store changed location several times, and eventually most of its activities were transferred to the Morning Star Ranch, a Digger rural commune.

18. **(c)** The Fillmore booked rock bands that later became world-famous. Among them were Big Brother and the Holding Company, the Paul Butterfield Blues Band, the Jefferson Airplane, Country Joe and the Fish, and the Grateful Dead.

19. **(c)** Khe Sanh, a small town near the Laotian border, was the site of a strategic U.S. Marine outpost. When U.S. Marines sighted and killed a group of North Vietnamese officers nearby, American commanders knew a major battle was brewing. A siege began in January 1968, and American forces were trapped there under desperate conditions until late March, when the North Vietnamese retreated into Laos.

20. **(d)** In 1960 the Belgian Congo, later renamed Zaire, achieved independence. However, when the mineral-rich Katanga area threatened to secede, civil war broke out. Katanga was forcibly reunited with the rest of the country in 1964 with the aid of UN troops. Before 1960 Rwanda was part of a trust territory with Burundi called Rwanda-Urundi. In January 1961 the country declared itself a republic and split from Burundi, and in July independence was granted.

21. **(b)** These countries all sent troops to Vietnam, but in most of them, the war eventually became as unpopular as it was in the United States. In 1967 an unofficial International Tribunal on War Crimes, held in Sweden, condemned the United States for atrocities in Vietnam and named Australia, New Zealand, and South Korea as accomplices. Australia and New Zealand began sending advisers in 1964 and troops in 1965, the year that South Korea first sent troops. Thailand sent troops in 1967. The combined loss of life for troops from Australia and New Zealand was 475; South Korea lost 4,407, and Thailand lost 350. In comparison, the casualties for U.S. troops approached 58,000. The Vietnamese death toll was far higher—over 185,000 South Vietnamese soldiers died, and North Vietnam lost over 900,000. In addition, at least 400,000 civilians were killed.

22. **(c)** Running on a Democratic platform calling for an end to the Vietnam War, the senator from South Dakota won only 35 percent of the popular vote, carrying only Massachusetts and the District of Columbia. McGovern would try and fail to gain renomination in 1984.

23. **(c)** The three-day festival was originally supposed to take place in Woodstock, New York, but the promoters ended up finding space on a farm near the village of White Lake; the nearest town of any size was Bethel, New York. In terms of population, for the three days of the festival the farm was the third largest city in New York State.

24. **(a)** With the withdrawal of France from Indochina in 1954, a provisional dividing line—including a demilitarized zone, or DMZ—was drawn across Vietnam at the 17th parallel. The original intent was to hold an election in 1956 with the ultimate aim of reuniting the country. Until then North Vietnam was to be governed by Ho Chi Minh, and South

Vietnam was to be governed by Emperor Bao Dai. Bao Dai appointed Ngo Dinh Diem premier, and, with U.S. support, Diem refused to hold the election. The DMZ became the scene of constant incursions by both sides in the late 1960s. With the reunification of north and south in 1976, the border disappeared.

25. **(a)** To protest segregation, the marchers planned to walk from Selma, Alabama, across the Alabama River and fifty-four miles along the Jefferson Davis Highway to Montgomery. On their first attempt, they were beaten and dispersed by police officers. On a later attempt they made it all the way to the state capital.

26. **(b)** The Freedom Rides were an effort to end segregation on intercity buses. The first Freedom Ride left Washington, DC, on May 4, 1961. The white and black riders planned to travel through Virginia, North Carolina, South Carolina, Alabama, Mississippi, and Louisiana. In Alabama the buses were attacked and burned. New buses were obtained, and the riders continued, but they were later stopped again and beaten by angry whites. Future rides traversed the whole distance.

27. **(c)** "Ole Miss," the University of Mississippi, is located in Oxford. When James Meredith enrolled as its first black student in 1962, riots by white students and townspeople focused the nation's attention on this Southern town.

28. **(b)** Birmingham, the largest city in Alabama, had a black population of about 140,000 in the 1960s. It made news for the attacks on Freedom Riders in 1961 and as the site of a lengthy series of demonstrations led by Martin Luther King, Jr.

29. **(d)** From the late 1950s into the 1970s, the CIA directed and financed a secret army in Laos that worked on espionage missions, sabotage, and assassinations. It was originally made up of local tribesmen called Meos, but so many Meos were killed that the CIA resorted to importing fighters from Thailand and other nations in Southeast Asia. In 1970 the existence of the secret army was revealed to the public, and Congress passed a law forbidding such an army. The CIA renamed the Thai troops "Laotian volunteers" and continued to fund them well into the 1970s. Concurrent CIA covert operations in other parts of the world, many of which were not discovered until much later, involved coups in Brazil and the Dominican Republic, destabilization of governments in Ghana and Nigeria, and the assassination of deposed Premier Patrice Lumumba in the Congo. The revelation of the CIA's role in Chile in the early 1970s was perhaps the biggest scandal affecting the agency at the time. Many attempts were then made to limit the CIA's power.

30. **(c)** When Vietnam was reunited, the former capital of the south was renamed after the late leader of the north.

31. **(d)** Jamaica became an independent member of the British Commonwealth in August 1962. Trinidad and Tobago won independence the same month. Barbados gained independence in 1966. All three new nations had been part of the British Empire, and their independence was typical of the worldwide decolonialization of the times. Other Caribbean islands that became free states within the British Commonwealth during this time included Antigua, Dominica, Grenada, St. Kitts-Nevis-Anguilla, St. Lucia, and St. Vincent.

32. **(a)** Following the assassination of Martin Luther King, Jr., the Southern Christian Leadership Conference, now led by Ralph Abernathy, went ahead with King's planned Poor People's Campaign, culminating in a "tent-in" on the Mall in Washington, DC.

33. **(b)** Max's Kansas City was an enormously popular bar and restaurant in the New York City hip scene of the late 1960s and early 1970s. The owner, Mickey Ruskin, at various times owned the Tenth Street Coffee Shop, Les Deux Mégots, the Annex on Avenue B, Ninth Circle, and One University Place. Max's mixed the downtown art crowd with Park Avenue types and mingled true hippies with Andy Warhol followers and Hollywood stars. The bar served as a gallery for artists whose work Ruskin chose to display, and live music was played upstairs.

34. **(c)** The Dom was a bar located in the Polish National Hall near St. Mark's Place and owned by Stanley Tolkin, who also owned Stanley's and the Gymnasium. Andy Warhol rented the top floor for an art Happening, "The Exploding Plastic Inevitable." The exhibit included music by the Velvet Underground, a light show, ongoing film clips, and dance. This upstairs dance hall, transformed into The Electric Circus, became the model for the discos of the 1970s. The Fugs were one band that got their start at the Dom-Electric Circus.

35. **(a)** The Village Vanguard featured jazz as well as comic acts. Unlike the other clubs featured on this map, the Vanguard is still in operation.

36. **(d)** The Psychedelicatessen sold drug paraphernalia and other hippie esoterica in the East Village in the mid- to late 1960s.

37. **(c)** Washington Square Park, surrounded by New York University, was the scene of early protests when folk music was banned there. The Washington Square Outdoor Art Show was and is an annual phenomenon, and the fountain and arch remain favorite places to hang out, buy drugs, or watch performances of all kinds.

38. **(a)** Vientiane is the capital of Laos. The three provinces mentioned were near the border separating North and South Vietnam and thus saw a great deal of fighting during the Vietnam War.

39. **(b)** Fort Bragg is an army training center in North Carolina. Camp Pendleton and Camp Lejeune are Marine Corps facilities in California and North Carolina, respectively. With the escalation of the Vietnam War, these bases were frequently in the news either as troop training camps or as focuses of protest.

40. **(d)** The story of African independence is enormously complicated and can only be understood in the context of the cold war. All of the countries listed had been under British control before the decade began. The dates of independence are as follows: Nigeria, 1960; Sierra Leone, 1961; Uganda, 1962; Kenya, 1963; Zambia (formerly Northern Rhodesia), Tanzania (formerly Zanzibar and Tanganyika), and Malawi (formerly Nyasaland), 1964; Zimbabwe (formerly Southern Rhodesia) and Gambia, 1965; and Lesotho (formerly Basutoland), 1966. Many Western countries, including the United States, had interests to protect in the new countries; and the CIA was enormously busy throughout the decade attempting to thwart Communist aid and left-leaning movements, whether this meant aiding tribal secessionists, as in Nigeria, or assisting in government overthrows, as in Ghana.

The Medium Is the Message: Art, Performance, and Media

I read the news today, oh boy...

—JOHN LENNON AND PAUL McCARTNEY

1. What happened in a Happening?

   a. Participants took LSD to help them see art in a new way.

   b. Improvisational drama led to street violence.

   c. The experience culminated in an onstage orgy.

   d. The audience became part of the art experience.

2. A 1969 film that involved a quest on motorcycles was entitled

   a. *The Wild One*

   b. *Easy Rider*

   c. *Help!*

   d. *American Graffiti*

3. What was the *East Village Other*?

   a. a play about aliens on the streets of New York

   b. a film directed by Andy Warhol and starring Viva

   c. an alternative newspaper focusing on the New York art scene

   d. an index of downtown artists compiled by Yoko Ono

4. Soft sculptures and Happenings were typical of the art of

   a. Claes Oldenburg

   b. Charles Henry Demuth

   c. Faith Ringgold

   d. Red Grooms

Sonnabend Collection, New York

5. This painting is typical of 1960s work by

   a. James Rosenquist

   b. George Segal

   c. Roy Lichtenstein

   d. Robert Indiana

6. The magazine *Ramparts* was best known for its
   a. emphasis on pop culture
   b. support of underground artists and filmmakers
   c. literary criticism
   d. political point of view

7. *Ice*, an early 1970s underground film set in the near future, featured
   a. Jane Fonda portraying a narcotics addict
   b. imaginative scenes of postnuclear destruction
   c. footage showing daily life in the Haight-Ashbury
   d. Weathermen and other radicals in leading roles

8. For what was the Bread and Puppet Theater known in the 1960s?
   a. guerrilla theater on political and social issues
   b. children's theater from a feminist perspective
   c. developing a "national underground theater" in Canada
   d. brilliant restagings of classic drama

9. The theater group El Teatro Campesino is affiliated with
   a. Cuban emigrés
   b. the United Farm Workers
   c. the Peace Corps
   d. the Third World Collective

10. *Feds and Heads* was the name of a(n)
   a. commune of artists
   b. unofficial directory of the underground
   c. play by Megan Terry
   d. comic book

11. With the 1971 publication of the Pentagon Papers, Americans learned of

  a. U.S. support of the assassination of South Vietnam president Ngo Dinh Diem

  b. President Lyndon Johnson's secret plans to escalate the Vietnam War

  c. a government cover-up of failed policies in Vietnam

  d. all of the above

12. The White Panthers were known for

  a. fighting for the rights of older Americans

  b. filming documentaries about the Black Panthers

  c. destroying a roomful of paintings in the Louvre

  d. art and performance tied to radical politics

13. Which of the following was a popular countercultural paper published in California?

  a. the *Los Angeles Times*

  b. the *San Francisco Examiner*

  c. the *Berkeley Barb*

  d. the *Rat*

14. A typical Yoko Ono work, "Cut" (1966), involved

  a. paper collage on a backdrop of the American flag

  b. kinetic sculpture made of steel and copper

  c. audience members removing Ono's clothing with shears

  d. an experimental film adaptation of *Othello* from Desdemona's point of view

15. Jules Feiffer is known for his plays and his

  a. cartoons

  b. films

  c. interviews with underground radicals

  d. all of the above

16. What was Fluxus?

    a. a movement of radical artists dedicated to demystifying art

    b. a collective of mescaline-influenced poets in San Francisco

    c. the name of a series of art shows held in Washington Square Park

    d. the organization responsible for the New Realist show

17. The Living Theatre was founded by

    a. the New York chapter of NOW

    b. Judith Malina and Julian Beck

    c. Jean Cocteau

    d. Joseph Chaikin

18. What did these artists have in common: Peter Max, Wes Wilson, and Victor Moscoso?

    a. The three developed the first alternative art school.

    b. Their art revolved around antiwar themes.

    c. They all created posters.

    d. They regularly created cover art for *Ramparts.*

19. Ads for the 1967 musical *Hair* referred to

    a. "Broadway's first all-nude revue"

    b. "the American tribal love-rock musical"

    c. "the unbelievable underground experience"

    d. "the hippest show in town"

20. What did the television programs "Laugh-In" and "The Smothers Brothers Comedy Hour" have in common?

    a. Both took their themes and style from the counterculture.

    b. Both were canceled because of censorship.

    c. Both featured comedienne Goldie Hawn.

    d. all of the above

21. The San Francisco Mime Troupe is known for performing
- **a.** nude
- **b.** in the streets and parks of the city
- **c.** exclusively in Spanish
- **d.** on the floor of the 1968 Democratic convention

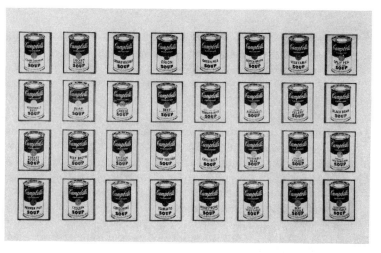

Private Collection of Irving Blum

22. Who painted this work?
- **a.** Henry Geldzahler
- **b.** Andy Warhol
- **c.** Roy Lichtenstein
- **d.** Billy Name

23. The street theater group called the Motherfuckers advocated which of the following?

   a. neo-Nazism

   b. creative violence

   c. Maoism and Buddhist principles

   d. flower power

24. What school of art does this work exemplify?

   a. op art

   b. pop art

   c. abstract expressionism

   d. silk screening

25. To whom did Liberation News Service provide news items and information?

   a. the third-world press

   b. New York art magazines

   c. the left-wing press

   d. local SDS chapters

26. Which architect was an early proponent of the geodesic dome?

    a. Howard Roark

    b. Frank Lloyd Wright

    c. Louis Sullivan

    d. Buckminster Fuller

27. Which magazine did Gloria Steinem found?

    a. the *Rat*

    b. *Ms.*

    c. *Other Scenes*

    d. *New Left Notes*

28. What artist drew this cartoon?

    a. the creator of *Zap Comix*

    b. Dr. Timothy Leary's lab assistant

    c. the head of the San Francisco branch of the Yippies

    d. the star of several of Andy Warhol's movies

29. What were "earthworks"?

  a. art forms that incorporated elements of nature

  b. dome-shaped houses built of mud

  c. street theater performances intended to promote ecological awareness

  d. mystical dramas that speculated on the origin of the earth

30. What happened at the *Rat* magazine in February 1970?

  a. The Weathermen accidentally set off a bomb.

  b. It was raided by the FBI and six editors were arrested.

  c. Several editors were found dead of heroin overdoses.

  d. Radical feminists took it over and produced an all-women's issue.

31. What characterized the films made by Jean-Luc Godard in the late 1960s?

  a. They starred only young, unknown actors.

  b. They used political radicalism as a backdrop to their plotlines and visual images.

  c. They addressed the audience directly.

  d. They devoted hours to showing slight changes in a single object.

32. What was *IT*?

  a. the Internal Theater, a Berkeley acting company

  b. the Illegal Troubadours, a street mime group

  c. the *International Times*, a London-based newspaper

  d. Intelligent Television, a countercultural TV station

33. What role did television play in the growth of the antiwar movement?

  a. It brought a true picture of the war into America's living rooms.

  b. It televised antiwar demonstrations.

c. It presented a nightly body count of dead and wounded.

d. all of the above

34. Which of these films was *not* directed by Andy Warhol?

a. *Chelsea Girls*

b. *Vinyl*

c. *Knife in the Water*

d. *Screen Test*

35. Which of the following was the first underground news-paper of the 1960s?

a. the *Open Process*

b. the *Los Angeles Free Press*

c. the *San Francisco Oracle*

d. *Up from Under*

36. What was the name of the experimental theater group founded by Joseph Chaikin and Peter Feldman in 1963?

a. Theater Genesis

b. Ridiculous Theater Company

c. Gut Theater

d. the Open Theatre

37. Why was the 1961 film *If* important to the countercul-ture?

a. It portrayed a rebellion against authority.

b. It showed a world without Establishment authority.

c. It portrayed the United States after a nuclear war.

d. It showed the result of a proletarian revolution in the United States.

38. The play *MacBird!* is about

a. a hallucinogen-inspired orgy

b. the dangers of nuclear weapons

c. Lyndon and Lady Bird Johnson

d. the Democratic convention of 1968

39. Paintings by Allan D'Arcangelo and James Rosenquist protested

   a. bigotry in America

   b. American militarism

   c. the mindlessness of pop art

   d. the oppression of the poor

40. Which of these 1960s movies portrays a mythical struggle between Establishment and anti-Establishment forces using psychedelic colors and rock music?

   a. *Tell Me Lies*

   b. *Kiss*

   c. *Yellow Submarine*

   d. *Weekend*

TEST 6: Explanatory Answers

1. **(d)** A loosely defined artistic event, a Happening melded art and performance, in which the audience was invited to participate. Happenings were begun in the early 1960s by such artists as Claes Oldenburg, Allan Kaprow, and Lucas Samaras. Later, Happenings became more free-form, and drugs and music eclipsed art as the central theme.

2. **(b)** In this film directed by Dennis Hopper, Hopper and Peter Fonda play small-time drug dealers who take off across the country in search for the underlying real America. They encounter commune dwellers, take LSD, and are finally killed by rednecks on a lonely Southern stretch. The film was extremely popular and gave rise to a rash of copycat versions.

3. **(c)** *EVO* was founded by John Wilcock in 1965 and run by Don Katzman, his brother Allan, and Walter Bowart. Features focused on poetry, art, and social and political life in downtown New York. Ronald Sukenick, in *Down and In* (1987), reports on Katzman's involvement in the forming of the Yippies and on *EVO*'s difficulties with the FBI.

4. **(a)** Oldenburg became known in the 1950s for his Happenings and in the early 1960s for installations such as *The Store* (1962), through which the audience could move freely. His plasters and soft sculptures of food include *Giant Hamburger* (1963) and *Soft Fur Good Humors* (1963), which simultaneously celebrate fast-food ingenuity and render it grotesque.

5. **(c)** Lichtenstein began as an abstract expressionist but became famous for his enlargements of panels from comic strips. These generally focus on a moment of tension and drama, as in this example, *Eddie Diptych* (1962). Lichtenstein was not the only artist of the time to explore the pop iconography of comics; Robert Rauschenberg, Andy Warhol, and Mel Ramos also chose to glorify images from comic strips in the early 1960s.

6. **(d)** *Ramparts* was founded in 1962 by Edward M. Keating as the "Catholic layman's quarterly," with the goal of reforming the Catholic Church. When it was taken over by *San Francisco Chronicle* editor Warren Hinckle III, it became a slick political monthly. Among its major stories were exposés of CIA involve-

ment in the National Student Association and of U.S. atrocities in Vietnam.

7. **(d)** *Ice*, filmed at the start of the 1970s and directed by Robert Kramer, depicted a band of radicals opposing an imagined future U.S. intervention in Mexico. Some of the principal roles were played by actual members of the Weather Underground.

8. **(a)** Peter Schumann founded the Bread and Puppet Theater, which became famous for its massive puppets and symbol-laden guerrilla theater. The theater performed on campuses and in the streets at many of the major demonstrations of the 1960s. It continues to be involved in political protest today.

9. **(b)** El Teatro Campesino performs skits and music about the lives of migrant farmworkers. It is an extremely popular and highly successful troupe and has managed to dramatize the plight of the farmworkers perhaps better than any pamphlets or articles could.

10. **(d)** *Feds and Heads* was the first underground comic book by Gilbert Shelton, who had achieved a following with his Wonder Wart-Hog series for the magazine *Help!* In 1967 Shelton created the Freak Brothers: Frankling, Fat Freddy, and Phineas. These sex-obsessed, pot-smoking hippies entertained readers of the *Los Angeles Free Press*, and Shelton based his comic book on their exploits.

11. **(d)** The Pentagon Papers were a study commissioned by Secretary of Defense Robert McNamara on U.S. involvement in Southeast Asia. The forty-seven-volume study covered policy decisions by the government from 1945 to 1968. Military strategist Daniel Ellsberg contributed to the study and then passed it to *New York Times* reporter Neil Sheehan in March 1968. The documents were, of course, classified, and the *Times* faced a daunting legal battle if it published them. Nevertheless, on June 13, 1971, the *Times* began publishing a series of articles based on the study. The White House immediately sought an injunction to bar publication, but the ruling was overturned on appeal, and the case moved to the Supreme Court. On June 30 the Court upheld the appeal, and publication of the papers resumed. Their record of government lies and illegal activities helped speed U.S. withdrawal from Vietnam by further reducing support for the war. Ellsberg was

charged with espionage and theft, but the charges were later dismissed.

12. **(d)** The White Panther party emerged from the Detroit Artists' Workshop in 1968. The White Panthers encouraged the widespread use of drugs and believed that rock and roll had the power to change the world. One of their leaders, John Sinclair, was arrested for giving marijuana to a narcotics agent and wrote a series of manifestos from prison. Performances were likely to include fake assassinations at poetry readings and music by the "house band," the pre-punk rock group MC5.

13. **(c)** In 1965, Max Scherr sold his Los Angeles bar to raise money to found a newspaper that would compete with the *Los Angeles Free Press*. The *Berkeley Barb* began by reporting on antiwar demonstrations and the Free Speech Movement, but it gained fame for reporting on the Berkeley/Haight-Ashbury social scene and local musical events. It had pages of rock criticism and informational columns on drugs and sex. It rapidly gained a wide audience—circulation peaked at 90,000 in 1969—and became one of the foremost alternative newspapers in the United States.

14. **(c)** Yoko Ono and her then-husband, Japanese electronic composer Toshi Ichijanagi, held a series of loft concerts in the early 1960s in which they explored music and theater, a mixture that later became known as performance art. In "Cut," first given at London's Destruction in Art Symposium in 1966, Ono knelt silently for an hour in the center of the stage as members of the audience cut away her clothing.

15. **(a)** Jules Feiffer published his first *Village Voice* cartoon in 1956. As that paper's circulation grew, Feiffer became known for his weekly sociopolitical drawings. Feiffer's dramas, including the black comedy *Little Murders* (1965), are similar to his cartoons in their exploration of a neurotic liberal America.

16. **(a)** Fluxus arose as a loose group of musicians and performers, some of whom studied with John Cage at the New School in the late 1950s. One of these artists, George Maciunas, planned a magazine that he decided to call *Fluxus*. Maciunas moved to Germany in 1961, where he met Nam June Paik and other avant-garde artists. A series of performance art pieces were

designed to promote the magazine, and these led to "propaganda actions"—demonstrations against "serious culture." Fluxus became the name for a movement dedicated to redefining art, merging the various disciplines into a new, action-oriented form. SoHo became the center of Fluxus when Maciunas moved back to New York, and Fluxus continued to sponsor performances and plan an artistic utopian community that was never realized.

17. **(b)** The Living Theatre was founded in 1947 by Julian Beck and his wife, Judith Malina. The group stressed a sense of community in which actors and other theater members lived and worked together. They gained attention with their radical political theater, but in 1963 they faced imprisonment for nonpayment of taxes and were forced to leave the country. Their work throughout Europe increased their fame, and they returned to the United States in 1968 to present a collective creation called *Paradise Now*. The techniques used by the group to expand improvisations and exercises into performances profoundly influenced theater around the world.

18. **(c)** Wes Wilson and Victor Moscoso gained fame throughout the San Francisco Bay area by creating posters for rock dance-concerts at the Fillmore and the Avalon. Wilson's posters were so popular that concert promoter Bill Graham was forced to give them away to concertgoers or risk having them all torn down. Wilson used graphics originally seen in turn-of-the-century Viennese posters. Moscoso created posters that changed under the changing colors of a light show, thus initiating a flood of "black-light poster" imitators. Peter Max made his fortune in New York with a psychedelic style that he translated into fabrics, accessories, and advertisements as well as posters.

19. **(b)** *Hair*, a musical by Gerome Ragni and James Rado, directed by Tom O'Horgan, opened Off-Broadway in November 1967. It told a story of a young man going off to war who is waylaid and saved by a tribe of hippies. Enormously popular for its rock score and minor nudity, *Hair* moved to Broadway in April of the following year, where it played 1,750 performances.

20. **(a)** The Smothers Brothers, Tom and Dick, had been a co-median-musician team for years when they finally got their own series. It featured a good deal of political material and some slightly racy jokes. The show lasted from 1967 until

1969, when battles with the censors knocked it off the air. "Laugh-In" began as a one-shot special in 1967. It had a psychedelic set and rapid-fire cuts that foreshadowed the video age, and it touched on political and social subjects. "Laugh-In" had a five-year run, twice becoming the number-one show. Its hosts were Dan Rowan (1922–1987) and Dick Martin, but it is better known for performers such as Goldie Hawn and Lily Tomlin, who parlayed their work there into successful acting careers.

21. **(b)** The San Francisco Mime Troupe was founded in 1959. Its director and main theoretician, R. G. Davis, set forth the goals of guerrilla theater: to teach, to direct toward change, and to be an example of change. The troupe adapts 17th-century plays in the *commedia dell'arte* form and presents them outdoors or in their own theater. During the 1960s the troupe became known for its association with the Diggers and with political groups—SNCC, CORE, and various antiwar organizations—performing frequently to raise money for these causes.

22. **(b)** Andy Warhol (1930–1987) was one of the foremost pop artists of the 1960s, headlining a movement that sprang up as a reaction to abstract expressionism. Pop art used the imagery of everyday objects to form a link between popular and high culture.

23. **(b)** The Motherfuckers, a highly visible presence on New York's Lower East Side in the 1960s, believed in a strange melding of dadaism, surrealism, and futurism. Led by, among others, a stepson of the famous leftist philosopher Herbert Marcuse, they became the Lower East Side chapter of SDS in 1968; and to promote anarchy, they dressed in black, smashed windows, set fires, and rallied to the cry "Up against the wall, mother-fucker!"

24. **(a)** Op (from *optical*) art was a sixties movement that attempted to make art a purely optical experience, without any meaningful associations. It was characterized by strong colors and pulsating patterns, often creating an illusion of movement.

25. **(c)** Liberation News Service was a press group that provided regular packets of photographs, articles, and cartoons to the various underground newspapers and journals during the 1960s. LNS was begun in 1967 by a group of writers and

journalists who had become revolutionaries. It was founded by Marshall Bloom, a graduate of Amherst, and Raymond Mungo. In 1968, LNS split in half along political lines: one faction fled to a commune in Massachusetts with the organization's money; the other half, Marxists, remained in New York. Both groups continued to send out news.

26. **(d)** The geodesic dome, designed by Buckminster Fuller, follows the dymaxion principle of maximum output from minimum energy and materials. Hippies popularized the design for dwellings during the 1960s because it was easy and inexpensive to build.

27. **(b)** *Ms.* magazine first appeared at the end of 1971 as a forty-page insert in *New York* magazine, where Gloria Steinem worked as an editor. It received so much attention that in January 1972 it was published as a one-shot issue, but 35,000 people wrote in requesting subscriptions, giving Steinem the money needed to get the magazine off the ground. *Ms.* has featured such writers as Susan Brownmiller, Susan Sontag, Nora Ephron, and Alice Walker. It has been criticized by some feminists as being "soft" on women's issues, but it continues to publish ground-breaking articles on rape, women's health care, and other related subjects.

28. **(a)** Robert Crumb began drawing comic book characters as a child. By 1966 he was living in the Haight-Ashbury and contributing regularly to underground newspapers. His first *Zap Comix* in 1967 began a new movement in comic art; his style was rough and somewhat sloppy, and he treated such popular subjects as sex and drugs. As well as the *Zap* series, Crumb developed Fritz the Cat, *Head Comix*, and *Motor City Comics.*

29. **(a)** Best illustrated by Robert Smithson's *Spiral Jetty* (1970), a sculpture of rock and salt in the Great Salt Lake in Utah, earthworks, or earth art, was an art form popular in the 1960s that used nature in its original forms.

30. **(d)** The *Rat* was a New York-based underground magazine known for its links to the Lower East Side radical group called the Motherfuckers. Offended by a series of misogynistic articles in the magazine, a group of feminists and Weatherwomen (as women members of Weathermen were then known) descended on the *Rat's* offices in February 1970 and took over the magazine for an issue promoting a guerrilla women's movement. Out of the issue came poet Robin Morgan's essay "Goodbye to All That," which reinterpreted revolution as a clash between men and women, asserting that women were the real Left. Eventually, the magazine became *Women's Liberation*, run by radical feminists.

31. (b) Jean-Luc Godard has gone through many stages in his career as a film director. From *Breathless* (1959) to *Two or Three Things I Know About Her* (1967) and *La Chinoise* (1967), his innovations in filmmaking have encompassed reductions of language, plot, and characterization, visual and auditory experiments, and political statements about the frustration and despair of the middle class.

32. (c) The *International Times,* renamed *IT* when Times Newspapers protested, was first published in 1966. By 1968 it was selling 50,000 copies per issue in England and the United States, but its preferences for personal introspection over political activism alienated many readers. In 1970 *IT* was prosecuted for conspiring to corrupt public morals because of the personal ads it printed, and the court costs closed the paper down.

33. (d) One of the major differences between the Vietnam War and America's earlier wars was the role of television. Since the conflict was not officially declared a war, there was little journalistic censorship. For the first time, Americans could see the difference between war propaganda and the horrible reality of war as shown nightly on their television sets.

34. (c) Though better known as a painter, Andy Warhol directed several underground films. Made on shoestring budgets, the movies featured nudity, drugs, and shots that lasted for up to half an hour. They help document a certain nihilistic spirit evident in the 1960s. *Knife in the Water* (1962) is directed by Roman Polanski.

35. (b) Begun in 1964, the *Free Press* included bright colors, daring cartoons, and articles on drugs and other countercultural subjects. The underground press, which by 1970 included hundreds of newspapers and magazines, helped shape the countercultural movement; it was the only forum in which all strands of the movement came together.

36. **(d)** In 1963, Joseph Chaikin and Peter Feldman founded the Open Theatre Company, whose work was based on improvisation taken to an extreme. Their best-known piece was *The Serpent* by Jean-Claude van Itallie, a story of the creation of man told through images of the assassinations of John F. Kennedy and Martin Luther King, Jr. With playwright Megan Terry, the group also performed *Comings and Goings* and *Viet Rock*.

37. **(a)** *If* is a British film starring Malcolm McDowell. It takes place in a boys' boarding school and portrays a student revolt against senseless authoritarianism. The film's popularity reflected the counterculture's empathy for such revolts and its distaste for the Establishment.

38. **(c)** *MacBird!,* a 1966 play by Barbara Garson, was a parody of *Macbeth* that portrayed Lyndon and Lady Bird Johnson as Macbeth and Lady Macbeth, deposing President Kennedy in order to escalate the war in Vietnam. The play was one of the greatest countercultural theater successes.

39. **(b)** Allan D'Arcangelo was a peace activist whose paintings often featured the eagle as a symbol of America's military strength. Many of James Rosenquist's paintings focused on the horrors of nuclear war, juxtaposing images of American consumerism with fighter planes or nuclear blasts.

40. **(c)** *Yellow Submarine* (1968) is an animated film by poster artist Heinz Edelmann that tells the story of the Beatles' battle against the Blue Meanies—obviously policemen—in the kingdom of Pepperland. The music is from *Sergeant Pepper's Lonely Hearts Club Band* and other Beatles albums.

Good Vibrations: Music

Everything we do is music.

—JOHN CAGE

1. What 1964 song was the Animals' biggest hit?

   a. "Bad Moon Rising"

   b. "Light My Fire"

   c. "House of the Rising Sun"

   d. "You Really Got Me"

2. Why was the Jefferson Airplane's 1967 song "White Rabbit" banned on some radio stations?

   a. It was an antireligion diatribe.

   b. It featured profanity.

   c. It was supposedly about drugs.

   d. It was about an incestuous relationship.

3. What rock-music-oriented publication did Jann Wenner start in 1967?

   a. *Spin*

   b. *Rolling Stone*

   c. *Rock News*

   d. *Billboard*

4. Who or what were the Fillmores?

   a. Janis Joplin's first band

   b. famous concert halls

   c. the guitars used by Jimi Hendrix

   d. backup singers for Sly and the Family Stone

5. What was Ravi Shankar's influence on rock and roll?

   a. He helped introduce the sound of Indian instruments.

   b. He was the first to use Burundi drums.

   c. He incorporated traditional Vietnamese melodies into his music.

   d. His songs included the slogans of third-world liberation movements.

6. What was new about the music of Sly and the Family Stone?

   a. It combined electric instruments with traditional orchestral instruments.

   b. It always included participation by the concert audience.

   c. It blended soul and rock into a crossover sound.

   d. It reinterpreted traditional folk songs with rhythm-and-blues arrangements.

7. When Country Joe and the Fish formed in 1965, what kind of music did they play?

   a. jug band music

   b. folk music

   c. country-and-western music

   d. rhythm and blues

8. Which of these bands melded beat poetry, rock music, and theater in their performances?

   a. Chicken Shack

   b. the Fugs

   c. the Byrds

   d. the Blues Magoos

9. Which of these bands did *not* play acid rock?

   a. the Grateful Dead

   b. Quicksilver Messenger Service

   c. Strawberry Alarm Clock

   d. Yes

10. What was Bob Dylan's first commercial hit song?

   a. "Lay Lady Lay"

   b. "Chimes of Freedom"

   c. "Like a Rolling Stone"

   d. "A Hard Rain's A-Gonna Fall"

11. Which band recorded the 1968 hits "White Room" and "Sunshine of Your Life"?

    a. Iron Butterfly

    b. Cream

    c. the Grass Roots

    d. Jethro Tull

12. Which of these bands was a hit at Woodstock with a combination of African, Latin, and rock rhythms?

    a. Sha Na Na

    b. the Holy Modal Rounders

    c. Santana

    d. the Lovin' Spoonful

13. What singer headlined with Big Brother and the Holding Company?

    a. Janis Joplin

    b. Grace Slick

    c. Marianne Faithfull

    d. Judy Collins

14. Which of these popular 1960s folk songs were written by Pete Seeger?

    a. "Where Have All the Flowers Gone?" and "Turn! Turn! Turn!"

    b. "Talking Vietnam Pot Luck Blues" and "Ramblin' Boy"

    c. "Nutbush City Limits" and "The Ballad of the Yellow Beret"

    d. "Cathy's Song" and "Old Friends"

15. Which of these bands did *not* play at Woodstock?

    a. Sha Na Na

    b. Deep Purple

    c. Jefferson Airplane

    d. Canned Heat

16. Which of these performers was associated with Andy Warhol and his Factory?

    a. Phil Ochs

    b. Lou Reed

    c. Van Morrison

    d. Jeff Beck

17. Which of these songs was written by this artist?

    a. "One"

    b. "I Had a Dream"

    c. "Jennifer Juniper"

    d. "You Were on My Mind"

18. For what is John Phillips known?

    a. singing with the Mamas and the Papas

    b. writing "San Francisco (Be Sure to Wear Flowers in Your Hair)"

    c. getting arrested on a narcotics charge with his daughter

    d. all of the above

19. Which of these groups hit the charts with songs by Bob Dylan, Pete Seeger, and Gordon Lightfoot?

    a. the Rascals

    b. Creedence Clearwater Revival

    c. Blood, Sweat and Tears

    d. Peter, Paul and Mary

20. Why was the Beatles' album *Sergeant Pepper's Lonely Hearts Club Band* considered such a musical innovation?

    a. All of the songs were performed under the influence of drugs.

    b. Many of the songs were improvised.

    c. It contained messages for listeners when played backward.

    d. It was recorded on a four-track tape recorder.

21. The real name of the Beatles' "White Album" (1968) was

    a. *Revolver*

    b. *Magical Mystery Tour*

    c. *The Beatles*

    d. *Abbey Road*

22. Guitarist Jimi Hendrix played with a band called

    a. Electric Lady Orchestra

    b. Blue Cheer

    c. Big Brother and the Holding Company

    d. the Experience

23. Who performed the music for the 1968 film *The Graduate*?

    a. Simon and Garfunkel

    b. Mick Jagger

    c. the Mothers of Invention

    d. James Taylor

24. "The Warlocks" was the original name of

    a. the Grateful Dead

    b. the Four Tops

    c. the Beach Boys

    d. the Allman Brothers

25. The title character of the rock opera *Tommy* (1969) is a

    a. drug pusher who becomes a rock-and-roll star

    b. pinball player who becomes a cult leader

    c. Vietnam veteran who turns to Christ

    d. runaway who joins a hippie commune

26. "Alice's Restaurant," a popular song later expanded into a film, was written by

    a. Van Morrison

    b. Richard Fariña

    c. Marianne Faithfull

    d. Arlo Guthrie

27. A concert at the Altamont Speedway in California is often called "the end of the sixties" because

    a. it took place on December 31, 1969

    b. a spectator was murdered during the concert

    c. it was Jimi Hendrix's last performance

    d. the Rolling Stones disbanded shortly thereafter

28. Phil Ochs was best known as

    a. the lead guitarist for the Hollies

    b. a producer and founder of Motown Records

    c. a protest singer and songwriter

    d. the lead singer for Creedence Clearwater Revival

29. Which Rolling Stone is matched *incorrectly* with his instrument?

  a. Keith Richards—guitar

  b. Bill Wyman—bass

  c. Charlie Watts—drums

  d. Brian Jones—keyboards

30. *Farewell Angelina* (1965) and *Any Day Now* (1968) were albums recorded by

  a. Tom Rush

  b. Jackson Browne

  c. Joan Baez

  d. the Band

31. Members of the Hollies, the Byrds, and Buffalo Springfield teamed up in 1969 to form

  a. the Animals

  b. Crosby, Stills and Nash

  c. Fairport Convention

  d. Little Feat

32. What instrument does Richie Havens play?

  a. piano

  b. saxophone

  c. guitar

  d. sitar

33. One important outcome of the Monterey International Pop Festival of 1967 was

  a. the first major rock concert film

  b. a new law banning marijuana in public places

  c. the world's longest antiwar petition

  d. the formation of the Paul Butterfield Blues Band

34. Judy Collins and Tom Rush had hits with songs written by
   a. James Taylor
   b. Frank Zappa
   c. Quincy Jones
   d. Joni Mitchell

35. Berry Gordy, Jr., made music history by
   a. founding one of the largest black-owned corporations in America
   b. writing the first song to go platinum
   c. hosting the first rock-and-roll dance program on TV
   d. all of the above

36. The Byrds' early recordings are of a type of music called
   a. soul
   b. fusion
   c. rhythm and blues
   d. folk rock

37. The anthem of the civil rights movement is based on a gospel song once titled
   a. "I'll Be All Right"
   b. "Swing Low Sweet Chariot"
   c. "The Lord Will Make a Way"
   d. "One More River to Cross"

38. Jim Morrison of the Doors was arrested in March 1969 in Miami for
   a. selling heroin to an undercover agent
   b. exposing himself onstage
   c. statutory rape
   d. driving while under the influence of alcohol

39. Buffy Sainte-Marie wrote many

    a. Motown songs covered by Stevie Wonder and Mary Wells

    b. songs protesting the lot of the American Indian

    c. biographies of rock stars who died young

    d. songs that became anthems of the antiwar movement

David Gahr / TIME Magazine

40. Which of these 1967 hits was recorded by this singer?

    a. "The Happening"

    b. "Respect"

    c. "Bernadette"

    d. "You're My Everything"

TEST 7: *Explanatory Answers*

1. **(c)** The Animals, a British band formed in 1963, included Alan Price, Eric Burden, Bryan Chandler, John Steel, and Hilton Valentine. "House of the Rising Sun" was a number-one hit in 1964, and the band had other hits with "Don't Let Me Be Misunderstood" (1965), "When I Was Young" (1967), and "San Francisco Nights" (1967). After five years few of the original members were still with the band, and they broke up in 1968. The other songs are by Creedence Clearwater Revival, the Doors, and the Kinks.

2. **(c)** The Jefferson Airplane was a San Francisco group formed in 1965. Led by Paul Kantner, with Grace Slick on vocals, the band epitomized the Haight-Ashbury scene. Their sound was a mix of folk, jazz, blues, and rock, and their first two albums went gold. The song "White Rabbit," which begins, "One pill makes you larger / And one pill makes you small," was purportedly about drugs; but despite some controversy, it made the Top Ten in 1967. In 1972 the band faded, but it reappeared with the name Jefferson Starship in 1974 and is currently known as Starship.

3. **(b)** In November 1967, the first issue of *Rolling Stone* magazine was published in San Francisco. Begun by Jann Wenner, a Berkeley dropout, the magazine has featured such writers as Hunter S. Thompson and Timothy Crouse. In the 1960s, *Rolling Stone* was one of the foremost chronicles of the counterculture that surrounded the world of rock music. The magazine is now more than twenty years old and is reportedly worth more than $15 million.

4. **(b)** The Fillmores were concert halls owned by concert promoter Bill Graham. The Fillmore opened in San Francisco in 1965, and its success led to the opening of the Fillmore East in New York City three years later. Bands such as the Grateful Dead and the Jefferson Airplane performed at the Fillmores. In 1968, Bill Graham opened a new San Francisco dance hall, the Fillmore West. The Fillmores finally closed within a week of one another in the summer of 1971.

5. **(a)** In 1965, Beatle George Harrison went to India to study sitar with Ravi Shankar, a well-known Indian musician. While there, he met Shankar's guru and became interested in Indian

religion. Harrison brought back both the sound and the spiritualism of India when he returned; the song "Norwegian Wood" is the first Beatles song to feature the sitar. In 1967, Shankar toured the United States, playing to packed auditoriums. He performed at Woodstock, but when the Indian influence became linked with the drug culture, he disassociated himself from the rock scene.

6. **(c)** Sly Stewart (Sly Stone) formed the Family Stone in 1967. The band's first hit was "Dance to the Music" (1968), and they went on to record such hits as "I Want to Take You Higher" (1969) and "Hot Fun in the Summertime" (1970). Their songs made the pop charts as well as the rhythm-and-blues charts, and they performed at Woodstock. Their popularity lessened in the early 1970s, and after the advent of disco the group disbanded.

7. **(a)** Joe McDonald formed the jug band the Fish in 1965, and they released their famous "F-U-C-K" cheer that same year. In 1966 the band went electric, and their "Feel-Like-I'm-Fixin'-to-Die Rag," an ironic antiwar song, brought them fame. They appeared at the Monterey Pop Festival and at Woodstock, but in 1969 the group was arrested in Massachusetts for inciting an audience to lewd behavior after leading a large crowd in the "F-U-C-K" cheer. Their popularity waned soon thereafter.

8. **(b)** Formed in 1965 by two beat poets, Ed Sanders and Tuli Kupferberg, the Fugs were satirists who composed profane, absurd musical pieces ridiculing sex, rock, politics, and the middle class. They performed on the Lower East Side for several years and were also participants in the famous attempt to levitate the Pentagon during the 1967 protest march, chanting "Out, demons, out!" on the back of a flatbed truck. In 1968 they toured Europe, attempting unsuccessfully to visit Czechoslovakia so that they could masturbate in front of the invading Russians. Ed Sanders later wrote *The Family*, a best-selling account of the Manson Family murders.

9. **(d)** Acid rock, also known as psychedelic rock, began in San Francisco with bands such as the Jefferson Airplane, Quicksilver Messenger Service, and the Grateful Dead. The sound of acid rock was meant to reflect musically the experience of an LSD trip; it included electronic sounds, Indian influences, and improvisation. Yes played progressive rock.

10. **(c)** Born in 1941 as Robert Zimmerman, Bob Dylan recorded his first album in 1961. At first known as a folk singer, he achieved fame quickly and by 1964 played hundreds of concerts yearly. In 1965 he incorporated rock and roll into his sound, shocking some folk fans but gaining him many more followers than he lost. The song "Like a Rolling Stone" hit number two on the charts in 1965.

11. **(b)** When guitarist Eric Clapton left John Mayall's band, he joined with bassist Jack Bruce and drummer Ginger Baker in 1966 to form the all-British group Cream. Their music melded rock and blues, and although the band stayed together for only two years, their 1968 LP *Wheels of Fire* was the first official platinum album.

12. **(c)** Led by Carlos Santana, the band Santana was formed in 1967 in San Francisco. Their hit songs "Evil Ways" (1969), "Black Magic Woman" (1970), and "Oye Como Va" (1970) blended Afro-Latino sounds with rock rhythms, and the band produced a platinum album and several gold albums. Later, Carlos Santana released solo albums and experimented with other performers such as John McLaughlin, Herbie Hancock, and the Fabulous Thunderbirds.

13. **(a)** Janis Joplin (1943–1970) got her start singing in Texas nightclubs, but she didn't achieve fame until she joined Big Brother and the Holding Company in San Francisco in 1966. They were the hit of the Monterey Pop Festival, and their album *Cheap Thrills* went gold. Joplin left Big Brother in 1968, and in 1970 she was found dead from a heroin overdose. Her posthumous solo album, *Pearl* (1971), gave her her last number one hit, "Me and Bobby McGee."

14. **(a)** Born in 1919, Pete Seeger had his first success as a folk singer in association with the Weavers in the 1940s. In the 1950s he was blacklisted for his political opinions, but in the 1960s his popularity grew with the release of albums such as *Songs of Struggle and Protest* and *Dangerous Songs*. The Byrds recorded Seeger's "Turn! Turn! Turn!" in 1965 and made it a number-one hit. More recently, Seeger has been crusading and performing for various political causes, often with Arlo Guthrie. The other songs listed are by Tom Paxton, Bob Seger, and Paul Simon.

15. (b) From August 15 to 17, 1969, the Woodstock Music and Arts Fair took place in Bethel, New York. Over 400,000 people attended; there were three deaths and two births during the concert. Performers included Santana, Canned Heat, Sly and the Family Stone, Melanie, the Who, Jimi Hendrix, the Grateful Dead, Joe Cocker, Joan Baez, the Band, and Crosby, Stills and Nash, among others. A film of the event was made, and two albums of the music were released.

16. (b) In 1965 in New York, Lou Reed formed the Velvet Underground with John Cale, Nico, Sterling Morrison, and Maureen Tucker. They met Andy Warhol in Greenwich Village, and he had them perform at his film showings and as part of his multimedia show. Warhol designed the cover of their first album, *The Velvet Underground and Nico* (1967). In 1968 they ended their association with Warhol, and Lou Reed left the band in 1970. His solo career has moved from a heavy metal sound to collaborations with jazz musicians and New Wave artists.

17. (c) Donovan began his musical career on a British television program in 1965, and almost immediately his songs became hits. At the Newport Folk Festival that year, he was well received by American audiences; and by 1968 songs like "Wear Your Love Like Heaven" and "Mellow Yellow" were high on the charts. After 1969 his popularity waned; he has since written scores for several films and musicals. The other songs listed are by Harry Nilsson, John Sebastian, and Sylvia Tyson.

18. (d) John Phillips, together with his wife Michelle, Cass Elliot, and Dennis Doherty, formed the San Francisco-based band the Mamas and the Papas in 1966. In the next two years they had six hits, among which were "California Dreaming" and "Monday, Monday" (both 1966). They performed at the Monterey Pop Festival, but in 1968 the group disbanded; the Phillipses were divorced in 1970, and Cass Elliot died in 1974. John Phillips's flower-power song "San Francisco (Be Sure to Wear Flowers in Your Hair)" (1966) was a hit for Scott McKenzie. In recent years, Phillips and daughter MacKenzie have lectured on the dangers of drug use. They have also revived the Mamas and the Papas with Doherty and Elaine "Spanky" MacFarlane.

19. (d) Peter, Paul and Mary's first album was released in May 1962, and their first big hit was a cover of "If I Had a Hammer" by Pete Seeger. They made the charts with Bob Dylan's "Blowin' in the Wind" in 1963, which brought Dylan national recognition, and they produced other hits through 1970. Since then, they have played several reunion concerts, often in support of political or social causes.

20. **(d)** In 1967, when *Sergeant Pepper* was released, four-track recorders were just coming into use, allowing musicians to layer sounds one on top of another. The album's electronic sound and unified concept, as well as the structural complexity of songs such as "A Day in the Life" and the druggy overtones of "Lucy in the Sky with Diamonds," had tremendous appeal for listeners.

21. **(c)** *The Beatles*, released in 1968, was a double album with a white cover. John Lennon (1940–1980) met Paul McCartney in 1957, and McCartney joined Lennon's group, the Quarrymen. George Harrison joined them later that year, and the band's name changed to Johnny and the Moondogs. Stu Sutcliffe joined as bass player in 1959, and the name changed again to the Silver Beatles. The drummer, Tommy Moore, was replaced by Pete Best in 1960. The Beatles played in Germany in 1960 and 1961, usually doing already popular rock-and-roll tunes. Sutcliffe left the band, and McCartney took over as bass player. The Beatles were "discovered" in Liverpool in 1961 by Brian Epstein, who landed them a recording contract. Ringo Starr replaced Pete Best, and the group recorded "Love Me Do," which made it to the Top Twenty. The Beatles were world-famous by 1963, and when they made their debut in the States in 1964, Beatlemania was truly underway. They led the so-called British Invasion, which revolutionized the rock-and-roll scene. Experiments with film, specialized recording techniques, Eastern music, and electronic sound kept the Beatles one step ahead of everyone else throughout the decade. The "White Album" was one of their last albums together. In April 1970, Paul McCartney produced a solo LP and the Beatles officially broke up.

22. **(d)** Jimi Hendrix (1942–1970) played backup guitar for such blues artists as B. B. King and Wilson Pickett before forming his own band in 1965. The Jimi Hendrix Experience was created in 1966 for a tour of England. It featured Mitch Mitchell on drums and Noel Redding on bass. The Experience was not seen in the States until 1967, when they played at the Monterey Pop Festival. That performance, captured on film, made Hendrix a star. His best-known albums, *Are You Experienced?* (1967), *Axis: Bold as Love* (1968), and *Electric Ladyland* (1968), featured the Experience but the band dissolved in 1969. Hendrix put together an all-black band with the name the Band of Gypsies. His last concert was in August 1970, and he died in September of a barbiturate overdose.

23. **(a)** Paul Simon and Art Garfunkel first sang together as children, and as teenagers they had a hit with a song by Simon called "Hey, Schoolgirl" (1957). At the time they called themselves Tom and Jerry. The duo got back together in the early 1960s and recorded *Wednesday Morning, 3 a.m.* (1966) for Columbia Records. At that time their sound was a folk-rock amalgam, and they sang Bob Dylan tunes as well as Simon's compositions. "Sounds of Silence" from the album became a number-one hit as a remixed single, and the pair were on their way. *The Graduate* won director Mike Nichols an Oscar and introduced audiences to actor Dustin Hoffman. Simon's "Mrs. Robinson" hit the number-one spot and helped make the soundtrack album a hit as well.

24. **(a)** Guitarist Jerry Garcia played with Mother McCree's Uptown Jug Champions along with Bob Weir and Pigpen McKernan, who were to stay with Garcia through the days of the Warlocks and the Dead. The Warlocks performed at Ken Kesey's Acid Tests and lived in a commune in San Francisco. They changed their name to the Grateful Dead, and by 1967 were regular performers at the Fillmore and the Avalon Ballroom. Supported in part by Owsley Stanley and his LSD profits, the Dead began to tour nationwide in the late 1960s. They appeared at Monterey and at Woodstock. Founding members of the band included McKernan (1945–1973), Weir, Phil Lesh, Bill Kreutzmann, and Garcia.

25. **(b)** Pete Townshend, lead guitarist for the British band the Who, wrote his first rock opera in 1968. The Who performed it in its entirety only twice (once at the Metropolitan Opera House), but the album became a hit thanks to the song "Pinball Wizard." Members of the Who included Townshend, Roger Daltrey, John Entwistle, and Keith Moon (1947–1978).

26. **(d)** "Alice's Restaurant" was performed at the Newport Folk Festival in 1967, and the song made Arlo Guthrie one of the

era's most popular folksingers. The song told of an arrest for littering, a trip to an induction center, and a woman named Alice who lived in a church and ran a restaurant. It was played repeatedly on underground radio and was immediately a major hit. The son of Woody Guthrie, Arlo maintained his father's folk tradition and inherited his political activism. The film *Alice's Restaurant* (1969) was directed by Arthur Penn and starred Arlo, James Broderick, and Pat Quinn as Alice.

27. **(b)** The Rolling Stones sponsored a free concert at the Altamont Speedway in Livermore, California, on December 6, 1969. Performers included the Stones, Santana, and the Jefferson Airplane. The Stones hired Hell's Angels to control the crowds, and this led to tragedy when an 18-year-old was stabbed to death by a Hell's Angel in front of the stage. The incident was captured on film, but the Angel was later acquitted. There had been three deaths from natural causes at Woodstock, but the violent undertones at Altamont led to public vilification of rock festivals across the country.

28. **(c)** Among the songs of Phil Ochs (1940–1976) are "I Ain't Marchin' Anymore," "Draft Dodger Rag," and "Outside of a Small Circle of Friends." He worked the Greenwich Village circuit in the early 1960s and wrote songs that were recorded by Joan Baez and other folksingers. His music was banned from the airwaves, but he was a hero to the antiwar movement.

29. **(d)** Brian Jones (1942–1969) played guitar with the band from its formation until he left in 1969 citing artistic differences. Mick Taylor was his replacement. Less than a month later, Jones was found dead in his swimming pool. The Rolling Stones—Richards, Wyman, Watts, Jones, and Mick Jagger—began playing together in 1962 and achieved a measure of fame surpassed only by the Beatles during the era of the British Invasion. Richards's and Jagger's number-one hits of the 1960s included "Time Is on My Side" (1964), "Satisfaction" (1965), and "Paint It Black" (1966–1967). They prided themselves on a certain raunchiness, answering the Beatles' "I Wanna Hold Your Hand" with "Let's Spend the Night Together" (1967) and "Let It Be" with "Let It Bleed" (1969).

30. **(c)** Joan Baez's first major concert was the 1959 Newport Folk Festival. She and her sister Mimi (who married author and folksinger Richard Fariña) started out singing traditional

folksongs, but Baez branched out to write songs of protest. She recorded songs by Bob Dylan and performed with him often from 1963 through 1965. She became heavily involved with the antiwar movement and donated her time and voice to rallies across the country, dramatizing the plight of draft evaders after her then-husband, David Harris, was jailed for refusing induction.

31. **(b)** David Crosby was with the Byrds from 1964 to 1967. Stephen Stills and Neil Young were with Buffalo Springfield, which often toured with the Byrds. Graham Nash was a founding member of the Hollies but quit that band in 1968. Crosby, Stills and Nash recorded their first album in 1969, and it won them a Grammy for such songs as Nash's "Marrakesh Express" and Stills's "Suite: Judy Blue Eyes." Neil Young began performing with the group midway through the year and was with them at Woodstock. His song about the tragedy at Kent State, "Ohio," was a hit in 1970, the year the group disbanded.

32. **(c)** Richie Havens is a black folksinger better known for his concert and outdoor rally performances than for his recording. Accompanied only by his own strummed guitar, Havens was featured at Newport, Monterey, the Isle of Wight Festival, and Woodstock.

33. **(a)** *Monterey Pop*, directed by James Desmond, is one of the most acclaimed concert films ever made, if only for performances by Otis Redding (who died in 1967), Janis Joplin, and Jimi Hendrix, among others. Attendance at the festival was approximately 50,000; thousands more saw the film, which was released in 1969.

34. **(d)** Joni Mitchell was known as a songwriter before she achieved fame on her own as a recording artist. In 1968 Judy Collins recorded "Both Sides Now" and Tom Rush recorded "The Circle Game." Their success paved the way for Mitchell's own. Her songs in the late 1960s ranged from the personal to the political and made her one of the nation's most popular solo artists.

35. **(a)** Gordy, a Detroit native, was a songwriter and automobile plant worker in the 1950s. He borrowed money from his sister to set up his own record production company and two labels

that later became Tamla and Motown. Gordy hosted talent searches throughout the Detroit ghetto and had an in-house team of writers create songs for the singers he found. Among Motown's performers were the Temptations, Smokey Robinson and the Miracles, Diana Ross and the Supremes, Marvin Gaye, and Stevie Wonder. Gordy's dream turned into an empire; his sister married Marvin Gaye, and his daughter married Jermaine Jackson (of the Jackson Five). Conflicts over artistic control caused some rifts in the Motown family, but the label had over 120 hits in the Top Twenty during the 1960s.

36. **(d)** In 1965 the Byrds took Bob Dylan's "Mr. Tambourine Man" and added a rock rhythm section, establishing what came to be known as folk rock. A second hit was Pete Seeger's "Turn! Turn! Turn!" Formed in 1964 in Los Angeles, the Byrds originally consisted of Roger McGuinn, Gene Clark, Michael Clarke, Chris Hillman, and David Crosby. By 1968 many of the original members had left, Gram Parsons (1946–1973) had joined the band, and the music they were playing was closer to country rock than folk rock.

37. **(a)** Pete Seeger first heard the song in 1947, when it was already being used as a protest song by striking tobacco workers. He added verses to the original and changed some words to create the song now sung around the world as "We Shall Overcome."

38. **(b)** Jim Morrison (1943–1971) was a poet who met keyboardist Ray Manzarek in film school at UCLA. The two began to write songs together and formed the Doors in 1965 with Robby Krieger and John Densmore. Their debut album contained the number-one hit "Light My Fire" (1967). Morrison was an exhibitionist with a serious drinking and drug habit, and his exploits kept the band in the news. His arrest in Miami for "lewd and lascivious behavior" was hardly his first, but the ensuing court proceedings interrupted the band's career. Morrison became a cult figure after his death in 1971, and his mix of sex, music, poetry, and drugs was widely imitated.

39. **(b)** Buffy Sainte-Marie, a Cree Indian, wrote songs and sang on the folk circuit, accompanying herself on guitar and mouthbow. Her first hit was "Universal Soldier" in 1964, which was remade by Donovan. Among her songs about American Indians are "Now That the Buffalo's Gone" and "My Country 'Tis of Thy People You're Dying."

40. (b) By the time "Respect" was recorded, Aretha Franklin had been recording hits for nearly a decade. She started out singing gospel with her sisters and father, touring the gospel circuit as a teenager, but by 1960 she was singing rhythm and blues. The year 1967 was key for her; she had changed labels from Columbia to Atlantic, and the recordings she made that year were hits on the pop charts as well as the R & B charts. To date she has more gold records than any other female vocalist. The other 1967 hits listed were recorded by Diana Ross and the Supremes, the Four Tops, and the Temptations.

Back to the Garden: Lifestyles

Never trust anyone over thirty.

—ABBIE HOFFMAN

1. Who was the Maharishi Mahesh Yogi?
   a. the divine spirit of Zen Buddhism
   b. a guru who preached Transcendental Meditation
   c. the American-born Hare Krishna leader who built a temple in West Virginia
   d. the founder of a cult headquartered in eastern Oregon

2. Augustus Owsley Stanley III contributed a vital element to the 1960s counterculture with his knowledge of
   a. architecture
   b. Sanskrit
   c. chemistry
   d. ancient folklore

3. Where was the hippie lifestyle centered in the 1960s?
   a. the Westwood area of Los Angeles
   b. New York's Lower East Side and San Francisco's Haight-Ashbury district
   c. the campuses of Berkeley and Columbia
   d. Greenwich Village in New York

4. Which of these was *not* an American Indian fashion adopted by 1960s hippies?
   a. beads and feathers
   b. fringed suede jackets
   c. headbands
   d. Mohawk haircuts

5. The "Summer of Love" in 1967 was
   a. a summerlong gathering in the Haight-Ashbury of thousands of young people from across the nation
   b. a series of nationwide demonstrations calling for the decriminalization of LSD
   c. an encampment at Taos, New Mexico, of converts to Eastern religions
   d. a monthlong rock-and-roll festival in upstate New York

6. The Earth Day observances of 1970 were planned by
   a. Women's Strike for Peace
   b. the Diggers
   c. environmental activists
   d. students at Columbia University

7. California's Esalen Institute became famous in the mid-1960s for conducting
   a. primal scream sessions
   b. sensory deprivation experiments
   c. encounter groups
   d. electroshock therapy

8. Hashish is closely related to
   a. peyote
   b. marijuana
   c. belladonna
   d. opium

9. The Diggers of the Haight-Ashbury dedicated themselves to
   a. the immediate establishment of a utopian community
   b. the building of Buddhist sanctuaries on Haight Street
   c. the publicizing of the "San Francisco sound" in rock music
   d. the manufacture of enough LSD to supply the whole country

10. Where did the Trips Festival take place?
    a. in Berkeley's "People's Park"
    b. in Central Park in New York
    c. in a longshoremen's hall in San Francisco
    d. on the beach in Santa Monica

11. Who named the hippies "hippies"?

   a. disgruntled beatniks

   b. *Time* magazine

   c. Johnny Carson

   d. John Lennon

12. What is an ashram?

   a. a recycling center

   b. a mystical phrase chanted repeatedly to induce spiritual bliss

   c. a page or chapter of a Zen text

   d. a Hindu retreat or school

13. What is a dashiki?

   a. a longhouse or other communal structure

   b. a loose-fitting Yoruba garment

   c. a tool used for dying fabric

   d. a personal spiritual guide

14. A huge gathering of hippies in San Francisco's Golden Gate Park in January 1967 was called

   a. "Haight Is Love"

   b. "The Death of Money"

   c. "A Tribute to Sparkle Plenty"

   d. "The Human Be-In"

15. The book *Our Bodies, Ourselves* was intended to

   a. awaken the nation to its nutritional deficiencies

   b. provide women with medical information

   c. establish a forum for gay and lesbian intercommunication

   d. teach acupuncture and shiatsu to doctors and nurses

16. Which of these is *not* a name for a kind of LSD?

   a. purple haze

   b. windowpane

    c. microdot

    d. psilocybin

17. Transcendental Meditation involved the use of

    a. mantras

    b. koans

    c. English translations of Hindu texts

    d. psychedelic drugs

18. Mescaline is the active substance in a drug produced from

    a. poppies

    b. mushrooms

    c. mandrake

    d. cacti

19. Who were the "Jesus freaks"?

    a. volunteers in the Christian Worker movement

    b. seven evangelists who established the Disciples of Christ

    c. draft evaders who based their pacifism on the Gospel

    d. converts or returnees to Christianity in the late 1960s

20. Dr. Benjamin Spock's influence on the counterculture included his antiwar activism and his

    a. books on organic farming

    b. designs for communal living

    c. relaxed attitude toward child rearing

    d. establishment of free clinics throughout the Bay Area

21. "Consciousness-raising sessions" were intended to

    a. prepare participants for the experience of communal living

    b. permit a free exchange of feelings and experiences

    c. free the mind of external pressures and inhibitions

    d. enable a meditator to approach satori

22. Dr. Timothy Leary began experimenting with hallucinogens while

    a. teaching transactional psychology at Harvard

    b. serving a five-year sentence for possession of marijuana

    c. visiting a commune in upstate New York

    d. researching Eastern philosophy at Berkeley

23. Which country produced this fashion look?

    a. the United States

    b. Great Britain

    c. France

    d. India

24. Which of these communes was *not* founded in the 1960s?

   a. Brook Farm

   b. the Hog Farm

   c. the Family of Taos

   d. Twin Oaks

25. Which of these drugs is a hallucinogen?

   a. Methedrine

   b. STP

   c. hashish

   d. PCP

26. What is the purpose of eating a macrobiotic diet?

   a. to ensure the survival of the human race

   b. to avoid refined foods

   c. to balance yin and yang

   d. all of the above

27. What effect did the Pill have on American society?

   a. It enabled people to get "high" legally.

   b. It lessened the incidence of sexually transmitted diseases.

   c. It permitted sexual enjoyment without fear of pregnancy.

   d. It led to the legalization of abortion.

28. What was the main type of product sold at a head shop?

   a. drug paraphernalia

   b. treatises on Eastern religions

   c. hippie makeup, headbands, and other accessories

   d. records of acid-rock music

29. What is the aim of yoga?

   a. simple healthful physical exercise

   b. feeling "high" without using drugs

   c. total relaxation of the body and mind

   d. spiritual realization and union with God

30. In 1967 many hippies believed they could get "stoned" by smoking

   a. tea leaves

   b. banana peels

   c. orange rinds

   d. sugar cubes

31. What countercultural enthusiasm did the song "The Age of Aquarius" reflect?

   a. women's liberation

   b. Hinduism

   c. astrology

   d. Taoism

32. What group was an unlikely part of the hippie scene from 1965 until the concert at Altamont?

   a. record company executives

   b. Bay Area computer programmers

   c. San Francisco socialites

   d. the Hell's Angels

33. What did the Maharishi Mahesh Yogi, Timothy Leary, and Trungpa Rinpoche have in common?

   a. They were all musicians.

   b. They were all considered gurus.

   c. They were all astrologers.

   d. They all believed in the spiritual power of LSD.

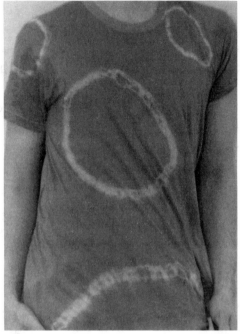

Cat Carter

34. What is this fabric print called?

   a. paisley

   b. Indian print

   c. tie-dying

   d. Nehru colors

35. What is the central feature of the practice of Zen Buddhism?

   a. meditation

   b. ingestion of consciousness-expanding drugs

   c. study of the teachings of Siddhartha

   d. renunciation of worldly goods

36. Who organized the first Acid Tests?

    a. Timothy Leary

    b. the Hell's Angels

    c. Ken Kesey and the Merry Pranksters

    d. the concert promoter Bill Graham

37. "Flower children" was another name for

    a. people who used LSD

    b. the Diggers

    c. the Yippies

    d. the hippies

38. For what is the *I Ching* used?

    a. predicting and interpreting events

    b. casting horoscopes

    c. analyzing personalities

    d. determining how to cook natural foods

39. Which of these is *not* a slang term for marijuana?

    a. maryjane

    b. weed

    c. smack

    d. dope

Cat Carter

40. What is the name of this article of clothing?

    a. army jacket

    b. Nehru jacket

    c. flak jacket

    d. Mao jacket

TEST 8: Explanatory Answers

1. **(b)** The Maharishi's brand of meditation, called TM for *transcendental meditation*, was just one of dozens of techniques adopted from Eastern religion in the 1960s by Westerners. The Maharishi gained international attention when the Beatles accompanied him to India in 1967 and announced their intention to give up drugs and follow his teachings. TM immediately became wildly popular, and posters of the Maharishi began appearing everywhere.

2. **(c)** Augustus Owsley Stanley III was a 29-year-old Berkeley dropout when he first tried LSD in 1964 and decided to become the master LSD chemist of all time. His first laboratory was in Berkeley; when it was raided by police, he moved to Los Angeles, where by May 1965 he was filling orders for LSD from around the country. Police surveillance sent Owsley running back to San Francisco, where he joined up with Ken Kesey and became the chief supply chemist for the Acid Tests. Along the way, Owsley made enough money to finance the rock group the Grateful Dead and the new San Francisco underground newspaper, the *Oracle*; his name became so well known that "Owsley acid" was the drug of choice for most acidheads. Owsley teamed up with a young chemist, Tim Scully, and the two maintained labs in the Haight-Ashbury and in Denver, manufacturing LSD in sophisticated tablet form and inventing new products, among them STP. Owsley was arrested in his lab in 1967 and sentenced to three years in jail. In *Storming Heaven* (1988), Jay Stevens describes Owsley's refusal to talk to the press throughout his trial on the grounds that he was merely a creation of the media, a media illusion. Others stepped in to fill the void in LSD marketing left by Owsley's arrest.

3. **(b)** Because housing was cheap and authority minimal, hippies flocked to the Haight-Ashbury district in San Francisco and to the Lower East Side, or East Village, in New York City. The scene in the Haight-Ashbury was very much in the public eye, especially after the 1967 Summer of Love: bands from the area such as the Grateful Dead and the Jefferson Airplane achieved national fame; Happenings such as the Acid Tests received extensive press coverage; and countercultural figures such as Bill Graham, Ken Kesey, and Augustus Owsley Stanley lived there.

4. **(d)** Mohawks came into fashion only with the punks of the late 1970s. Just as the beatniks had adopted certain aspects of the culture of black Americans, so the hippies seized on Native American culture as being more meaningful than their own generally middle-class upbringing. Their crosscultural borrowings included the wearing of deerskin moccasins, silver and turquoise jewelry, and headbands—and, of course, the practice of ingesting the hallucinogenic buttons of the peyote cactus. The hippies' back-to-nature movement was another outgrowth of their identification with Native Americans, as was the tendency to refer to communal groups as "tribes." Ken Kesey helped launch this interest with his character Chief Broom in *One Flew Over the Cuckoo's Nest* in 1962. The 1965 multimedia show "America Needs Indians" was a huge hit in San Francisco, the 1967 Be-In was referred to as "A Gathering of the Tribes," and later events planned for spring and autumn equinoxes and summer solstices often had Indian advisors.

5. **(a)** Following the success of the Human Be-In in January 1967, the San Francisco *Oracle* published an invitation to young people across the country to come to the Haight-Ashbury for a "Summer of Love"—and presumably take the hippie ethos back with them to wherever they came from. In anticipation, committees were formed to sponsor free events, centers for runaways were established, Bill Graham decided to stage concerts at the Fillmore six days a week, and reporters from the national press descended on the area in droves. When summer came, huge numbers of all kinds of outsiders converged on the Haight, causing many old-time residents to consider leaving the tourist-clogged area for other cities or rural communes.

6. **(c)** Earth Day was organized in New York City by a small group of people concerned about pollution and smog. On April 22, 1970, observances took place across the country. Some involved clean-up programs; others featured traffic blockades and car "funerals." The success of the day made it clear that a large number of people had switched their attention from the antiwar or civil rights movements to environmental concerns, and environmentalism would gain momentum through the 1970s.

7. **(c)** In the mid-1960s the Esalen Institute in Big Sur, California, became famous for its "human potential experiments" involv-

ing meditation and a form of group therapy called the encounter group. People from around the nation came to take part in these groups, which involved the open expression of feelings among people who might begin as total strangers. The goal was "personal growth," or becoming an honest, open person.

8. **(b)** Marijuana is derived from the leaves and flowers of the hemp plant. The resin from the female plant is used to make hashish, a more potent drug, usually smoked in a pipe.

9. **(a)** The Diggers, who took their name from a group of 17th-century English egalitarian revolutionaries, were utopian anarchists who did not fit any standard political definitions. Begun by Emmett Grogan and other members of the San Francisco Mime Troupe, they specialized in a combination of symbolic street theater and utopian activism—all based on the premise that the existing social order was obsolete and that it was time to move on to a higher stage in which everyone and everything would be absolutely free. To this end, each day they distributed free food to the Haight community from a soup kitchen in Golden Gate Park; they also opened "free stores" that stocked free clothing and other essentials. The embodiment of the Haight's early wild hope and enthusiasm, by 1967 they were warning of the co-optation and profiteering that would soon engulf the countercultural community.

10. **(c)** The three-day Trips Festival of January 1966 was the combined effort of Bill Graham, Stewart Brand, Ken Kesey and the Merry Pranksters, and a variety of other Haight-Ashbury regulars. It was held in Longshoremen's Hall in San Francisco and featured LSD, light shows, dance, cabaret theater, and the music of Big Brother and the Holding Company and the Grateful Dead. The audience was invited to participate and to wear "ecstatic dress." According to Tom Wolfe, "the Haight-Ashbury era was born that weekend."

11. **(a)** *Hippie* is a diminutive of *hipster*, a rather condescending term denoting the beats' disdain toward the newer countercultural folk who tended to use drugs for the sake of the experience rather than for the sake of art, and who preferred rock music to jazz. In *Storming Heaven* (1988), Jay Stevens attributes the term to *San Francisco Examiner* writer Michael Fallon in a 1965 article.

12. **(d)** An ashram is the home of a Hindu sage, where he lives and teaches his disciples. It may also refer simply to a retreat for meditation and prayer. As Eastern religion gained ground in the United States, ashrams sprang up in the countryside. Many of the faithful chose to visit India to study with gurus in their ashrams.

13. **(b)** The dashiki, a loose, flowing, brightly patterned garment from the African country of Guinea, became popular in the United States with the rise of the Black Power movement. A new interest in African culture led to various adaptations of African styles; also popular was the natural hairstyle sometimes called the Afro.

14. **(d)** The uniting of hippies with political radicals was one of the themes behind the first Be-In. Such disparate characters as Allen Ginsberg, Timothy Leary, and Jerry Rubin helped coordinate the event, in which some 10,000 people heard speeches, danced to music by San Francisco bands, chanted Hindu and Buddhist rituals, ate free turkey sandwiches (some laced with LSD), and generally celebrated the birth of the countercultural community.

15. **(b)** *Our Bodies, Ourselves* (1973) contains information on sexuality, nutrition, exercise, alternative treatments, childbirth, and self-defense, among other topics. The concept was born at a 1969 women's conference at which women's frustration with the health care industry emerged as a major concern. A women's group in Boston began teaching a course on women's health issues, and the course proved so popular that its spiral-bound text, compiled by the Boston Women's Health Collective, was published commercially and became a nationwide best-seller.

16. **(d)** In 1943 in Basel, Switzerland, Albert Hoffman, a chemist at Sandoz Pharmaceuticals, synthesized a new compound, which he called LSD-25. He then took a very small dose. Later, when he tried to bicycle home, it became clear that the world had a new kind of mind-expanding drug. In the 1950s many psychologists viewed LSD as a valuable psychiatric tool, and it was widely studied. In the 1960s, however, underground chemists began making it widely available—with descriptive names such as purple haze, windowpane, and microdot—to the hippie community, which had other uses for it. It was not

made illegal until 1966. Psilocybin was Sandoz's name for a compound made from a Mexican mushroom, *Psilocybe mexicana*, whose psychedelic properties had been part of Indian rituals for centuries.

17. **(a)** Mantras are mystical formulas recited in Hindu and Buddhist meditation and other rituals to call into being the object or deity represented by that formula. Personal mantras may be given to a pupil by a guru, or groups of worshippers may chant a single mantra.

18. **(d)** Kiowa and Navaho Indians used the peyote cactus in religious ceremonies long before the powers of the plant were discovered by other Americans. The Aztec people had used peyote for centuries. The active substance that gives the cactus its hallucinatory power is called mescaline. The dried tops of the cactus are called peyote buttons, and it is this form of the plant that is most often used in rituals. In the 1950s mescaline became available in crystal form, usually powdered and inserted into capsules. Aldous Huxley popularized the drug with his 1954 essay *The Doors of Perception*.

19. **(d)** Disenchanted with Eastern religions and drugs but still searching for meaning and community, some people in the counterculture turned back to traditional Western culture and the teachings of Christ. "Jesus freaks" often lived communally, and some of the communes evolved into cults as the 1970s began.

20. **(c)** *Baby and Child Care* was first published in 1946, coinciding neatly with the start of the baby boom, under the title *The Common Sense Book of Baby and Child Care*. It remains one of the best-selling books of all time. Spock contradicted conventional child-rearing practices by stressing the individualism of each child and suggesting that the role of the parent is to provide reassurance and understanding. So many baby boomers were raised on Spock's book that they became known as the "Spock generation." In 1967 Spock left the medical field to work full-time for antiwar causes.

21. **(b)** After the feminist protest at the 1968 Miss America pageant, small "rap groups" of women began springing up around the country. In these groups women would talk about their experiences as women and discuss their feelings and personal

problems. "A Program for Feminist 'Consciousness Raising' " was a paper presented by Kathie Sarachild at a women's conference in 1968. In the paper Sarachild declared that such feelings were political rather than exclusively personal and that the primary task of such groups was to awaken a class consciousness in women—a recognition of women *as a class* that would lead to political action and change.

22. **(a)** Leary graduated from Berkeley with a doctorate in clinical psychology. He directed the research lab at the Kaiser Clinic, and then in 1959 he accepted a lectureship at Harvard. In August 1960, intending to work on a book, he went to Mexico, where he was introduced to hallucinogenic "magic mushrooms." The experience prompted him to establish the Harvard Psilocybin Project with colleague Richard Alpert to study that drug's potential therapeutic qualities. Initial experiments with convicts were encouraging, but in the middle of the project Leary tried some LSD. At that time LSD was known to many psychologists, but most were wary of it because LSD sessions were considered hard to control—"set and setting" were thought to be the key to a successful "trip." To Leary, however, LSD was not just a therapeutic drug; it was something far more important, something he would later call a "door" leading out of "fake-prop-television-set America" and into another, higher plane of existence. Leary began using Harvard students in his experiments, but before long the university halted his work, and he and Alpert were fired. The two researchers then set up their own commune/ashram/research facility at Millbrook, New York, and Leary spent the rest of the decade wandering among Millbrook, India, and Mexico, with occasional appearances in court for possession of marijuana. In 1966 he founded the League of Spiritual Discovery, which espoused the sacramental use of hallucinogens. He lectured widely and held an ongoing open house for those who wished to learn about the powers of LSD. Alpert stayed in an Indian ashram for a year, emerging in 1968 as Baba Ram Dass.

23. **(b)** First introduced by British designer Mary Quant in 1960, the miniskirt took the fashion world by storm in 1962. The new style was sexy, but many women also considered it liberating: gone were confining girdles and garter belts. The Carnaby Street look—so called from the London street where many fashion boutiques were located—featured shirtwaist minidresses in polkadot or striped prints with a wide tie. Textured pantyhose was the appropriate legwear, and hair was short and straight.

24. **(a)** Brook Farm was a Massachusetts commune formed by the Transcendentalists in the 1840s. The idea of utopian communities has existed for centuries; first discussed by Plato, utopias were imagined by Rabelais, Bacon, Saint-Simon, and Sir Thomas More. In the 1960s the idea was reborn with a movement toward self-sufficient farming communities. Most people who joined communes at this time did so for ideological reasons: the idea of returning to the land and living independent of society had great appeal. However, most communes lasted no more than five years, dissolving because of disputes among members, money problems, or negative reaction from the neighboring community.

25. **(b)** STP, the common name for 2,5 dimethoxy-4-methylamphetamine, was first synthesized in the 1960s by a friend of the well-known LSD chemist Augustus Owsley. According to rumor, STP could keep you as high as LSD for three days at a fraction of the cost. However, bad trips on STP were common and sometimes irreversible. The drug's bad reputation eventually brought its use to a stop.

26. **(d)** People who follow macrobiotic diets do so as much for the survival of humanity on earth as for their own personal health. Macrobiotics is a blending of Eastern and Western philosophy, first brought to the United States from Japan by George Ohsawa, who was cured of tuberculosis by following strict macrobiotic guidelines. A macrobiotic diet consists of 50 to 60 percent grains, 20 to 25 percent vegetables, 5 to 10 percent beans and sea vegetables, and 5 to 10 percent soups. Food intake can be modified according to social conditions, personal needs, and climate, and other foods are occasionally allowed to promote the balance of yin and yang.

27. **(c)** First approved for marketing by the FDA in 1960, the birth control pill is a method of oral contraception that prevents pregnancy by inhibiting ovulation. It is 99 percent effective. As its use spread in the 1960s, women, free for the first time from the fear of pregnancy, were able to engage in sex more often and with more partners, ushering in the so-called sexual revolution.

28. **(a)** Head shops were among the first businesses to reflect the interests of the 1960s counterculture. The first head shop was the Psychedelic Shop, opened in the Haight-Ashbury in January 1966. Like those that followed, it sold bhangs, pipes, rolling papers, and other drug paraphernalia. The Psychedelic Shop also sold some literature, fabrics, and concert tickets.

29. **(d)** Yoga was developed more than 2,000 years ago in India. The word itself means "discipline," and followers of Buddhism and Hinduism practice it. There are many kinds of yoga: *Jnana-yoga* is the renunciation of the unreal; *karma-yoga* is the performance of duty; *bhakti-yoga* is the love of God; and *hatha-yoga* is physical exercise. *Raja-yoga*, one of the six systems of Hindu philosophy, remains popular in the United States. It stresses the liberation of the soul from the body. In the past, one who truly wanted to attain spiritual rebirth through yoga would have to withdraw completely from the world, but in the 1960s this stricture was relaxed.

30. **(b)** In March 1967, the *Berkeley Barb* reported that it was possible to get high by smoking dried banana peels. A friend of the rock band Country Joe and the Fish had discovered that banana peels contain norepinephrine and serotonin, chemicals involved in the synthesis of psychedelic drugs; thus, when smoked, the dried peels turn into a psychedelic chemical. Within a week, hippies could buy $5 bags of banana peel; shortly afterward, there was a mass Banana Turn-on at Berkeley. Needless to say, very few people ever got high by this method.

31. **(c)** Astrology, popular for thousands of years, gained new believers in the 1960s. The idea that the location of the stars and planets controls one's life coincided with the counterculture's search for spiritual guidance. Astrology is based on observations of the zodiac (twelve star constellations coinciding with the twelve segments of the year) and of the movement of the planets across the sky. According to this theory, when you were born determines to a great extent your personality, actions, and potential.

32. **(d)** In August 1965, Ken Kesey and his Merry Prankster friends, back from touring in their psychedelically painted school bus, invited the San Francisco chapter of the Hell's Angels motorcycle gang to a party at Kesey's home in La Honda. There

Kesey introduced the Angels to LSD, and the bikers were immediately converted. Soon the Angels were heavily involved in both the supply side and the demand side of the psychedelic drug trade. By the end of the 1960s, however, and especially after the 1969 Altamont concert at which an Angel stabbed a spectator to death, the group lost its appeal to the hippies.

33. **(b)** A guru is a spiritual teacher in the Hindu religion. The guru was a basic link in the chain of oral tradition and teachings that led to the knowledge of God. When hippies discovered yoga and Indian religion in the 1960s, they also discovered gurus. Some gurus of the era were genuine Indian mystics; but by the late 1960s, the term *guru* referred to any mystical teacher, including, for example, Dr. Timothy Leary. Trungpa Rinpoche was a Tibetan guru whose Naropa Institute in Boulder, Colorado, is still flourishing.

34. **(c)** Tie-dying was a way to be artistic using nothing but a T-shirt and a box of dye. To tie-dye a piece of clothing, you tied strings around clumps of fabric and then dyed the entire garment. When the garment dried and the strings were re-moved, the result was a psychedelic, sunburst effect.

35. **(a)** Brought by Bodhidharma to China in the fifth century A.D., Zen is a form of meditation that leads to satori, or "sudden enlightenment." Often, a student of Zen must meditate on a koan, or paradoxical saying. In later times, Zen became a great influence in Japan and was reflected in many aspects of Japanese culture: the art of the tea ceremony, flower arranging, and many classic Japanese poems are based on Zen. In the 1960s Zen was revived in the United States and found a great following in the counterculture.

36. **(c)** Ken Kesey took his first LSD trip in 1960 in a veterans' hospital as part of a government-approved experiment. By 1964 he and his Merry Prankster friends were traveling around the country in their Day-Glo-painted school bus, turning on themselves and the people they met. After a year they returned to San Francisco and began holding what they called Acid Tests: parties first at Kesey's home, then at bars, and finally at the Fillmore concert hall in San Francisco. At these gath-erings everyone who attended was given LSD, which was then still legal; at the later Tests music was provided by the Grateful Dead. In January 1966 the basic features of the Acid Tests were incorporated by concert promoter Bill Graham into the enormously successful three-day Trips Festival.

37. **(d)** A term coined by San Francisco newspapers in the mid-1960s, "flower children" reflected the innocence and childlike enthusiasm for new experiences possessed by the first influx of hippies into the Haight-Ashbury. As early as 1962 Allen Ginsberg referred to "flower power," which signified the power of nature to defeat war and suffering. Although at first the flower children of the Haight may have believed in flower power, by the late 1960s drugs and street living had taken their toll, and the innocent belief in the power of flowers had worn thin.

38. **(a)** The *I Ching*, or Book of Changes, was written 3,000 years ago in China. It contains a set of sixty-four hexagrams that symbolize different human situations, as well as explanations for each hexagram. For Taoists the *I Ching* is both a tool to aid in understanding and predicting events and a philosophical guide.

39. **(c)** Marijuana, which comes from the hemp plant, has many nicknames, as do most illegal drugs—and some legal ones, such as alcohol. Weed, smoke, reefer, pot, dope, and maryjane are some of marijuana's aliases. Possession of marijuana has been illegal in the United States since 1937. Smack is another name for heroin.

40. **(b)** Along with the influx of Indian music, Indian religion, and Indian philosophy came Indian fashion. Many women in the 1960s possessed at least one garment made from an Indian-print bedspread, and elaborately embroidered vests and shirts, some decorated with small mirrors, were popular. The Nehru jacket was a short-lived phenomenon; named after the first prime minister of India, Jawaharlal Nehru, it featured a notched collar and was often made in bright, multicolored Indian cottons.

The Word Is Love: Quotes, Phrases, and Symbols

Everything that is thought and expressed in words is one-sided, only half the truth; it all lacks totality, completeness, unity.

—HERMAN HESSE

1. Why did hippies refer to the 1960s as "the Age of Aquarius"?

   a. Aquarius is the astrological sign of peace.

   b. Aquarius is a water sign, and water symbolizes the essence of life.

   c. The astrological Age of Aquarius is to begin in 2000 A.D.

   d. The Age of Aquarius is supposedly when the young will inherit the earth.

2. Who called what event "the first attempt to land man on the Earth"?

   a. Jerry Rubin: the return of *Apollo 11*

   b. Abbie Hoffman: Woodstock

   c. Timothy Leary: the synthesis of LSD

   d. Hunter S. Thompson: the Summer of Love

3. Who stated, "I'm not going to be the first American president who loses a war"?

   a. Lyndon B. Johnson

   b. Richard M. Nixon

   c. John F. Kennedy

   d. Hubert H. Humphrey

4. Who originated the phrase "Up against the wall, Motherfucker"?

   a. LeRoi Jones

   b. Stokely Carmichael

   c. Allen Ginsberg

   d. Malcolm X

5. What does this figure symbolize?

   a. love

   b. the balance of yin and yang

   c. peace

   d. rebirth

6. The people who chanted "Dump the Hump!" wanted

   a. to save the humpback whales from slaughter

   b. Richard Nixon to win the 1968 election

   c. the Democratic party to nominate another candidate in 1968

   d. Lyndon Johnson to choose a different vice-president

7. Which organization drafted the statement that began, "We are the people of this generation, bred in at least modest comfort, looking uncomfortably to the world we inherit"?

   a. the Black Panthers

   b. Students for a Democratic Society

   c. the Yippies

   d. the Socialist Workers party

8. In what year did demonstrators chant "Haight is love"?

   a. 1965

   b. 1968

   c. 1969

   d. 1967

9. To what did the term "bummer" originally refer?

   a. a bad LSD trip

   b. a mental depression

   c. a riot

   d. the breakup of a relationship

10. Who originated the slogan "black power"?

   a. Stokely Carmichael

   b. Malcolm X

   c. Martin Luther King, Jr.

   d. H. Rap Brown

11. Fill in the blank: "Hey, hey, LBJ, _____ "

   a. "We'll bomb Vietnam if you have your way."

   b. "How many kids did you kill today?"

   c. "Integrate, integrate, integrate today!"

   d. "Stop the brutal murders by the CIA."

12. Who proclaimed that "violence is as American as cherry pie"?

   a. H. Rap Brown

   b. Bernardine Dohrn

   c. Tom Hayden

   d. Mark Rudd

13. To what event did the statement "It became necessary to destroy the town in order to save it" refer?

   a. the massacre at My Lai

   b. the murder investigation by the FBI in Philadelphia, Mississippi

   c. the air attack on Ben Tre

   d. Mayor Daley's violent response to the protests at the 1968 Democratic convention in Chicago

14. With what is this gesture associated?

   a. women's liberation

   b. voting rights

   c. the Weathermen

   d. the Black Panthers

15. Who said America could have "peace with honor" in Vietnam?

   a. John F. Kennedy

   b. Lyndon B. Johnson

   c. Richard M. Nixon

   d. Robert F. Kennedy

16. Who said about Vietnam, "We're going to bomb them back to the Stone Age"?

   a. General William Westmoreland

   b. Richard M. Nixon

   c. Lyndon B. Johnson

   d. General Curtis LeMay

17. What was the statement "Our country, right or wrong" meant to counter?

   a. the threat of communism

   b. protests against the Vietnam War

   c. the Voting Rights Act

   d. Watergate

18. What did this symbol represent to the counterculture?

    a. the Free Speech movement

    b. SDS

    c. the Stop the Draft movement

    d. Black Power

19. Who said, "Say it loud, I'm black and I'm proud"?

    a. James Brown

    b. Huey Newton

    c. Bobby Seale

    d. LeRoi Jones

20. Who defined a hippie as a person who "dresses like Tarzan, has hair like Jane, and smells like Cheetah"?

    a. Richard M. Nixon

    b. George Wallace

    c. Ronald Reagan

    d. Richard Daley

21. With what event is the chant "the whole world is watching" associated?

    a. police beating demonstrators at the Democratic convention in Chicago

    b. Yippies attempting to levitate the Pentagon during the 1967 Washington peace demonstration

    c. hippies cavorting in the mud at Woodstock

    d. Lyndon Johnson declining to run again for the presidency

22. The phrase "Burn, baby, burn" is associated with

   a. antiwar demonstrators attacking returning veterans

   b. uprisings in urban ghettos

   c. U.S. troops destroying Vietnamese villages

   d. Jack Kerouac

23. *Om* is a

   a. Tibetan word meaning "peace"

   b. name for God

   c. mantra

   d. term of respect used when addressing a guru

24. "Girls say yes to boys who say no" urged young men to say no to

   a. drugs

   b. sex without contraception

   c. college deferments

   d. military conscription

25. The phrase "speed kills" exhorts the listener to stay away from

   a. drunk drivers

   b. any product from Detroit

   c. Methedrine

   d. methadone

26. The phrase "flower power" refers to

   a. the ability of the earth to regenerate

   b. the hardiness of marigold seeds

   c. the power of nonviolence over violence

   d. faith in the thought that spring will come again

27. Fill in the blank: "Ho Ho Ho Chi Minh, _____"

   a. "NLF is gonna win."

   b. "Push 'em back to Gia Dinh."

   c. "Our GIs are gonna win."

   d. "Organize and smash the state."

28. The Black Panther leader Huey Newton ended many speeches with the phrase

    a. "All power to the people!"

    b. "Remember Malcolm, who died for your sins."

    c. "You are somebody."

    d. "To the barricades!"

29. What was the original meaning of this symbol?

    a. "End the war"

    b. "Peace and freedom"

    c. "Nuclear disarmament"

    d. "Stop, think, change"

30. "Injustice anywhere is a threat to justice everywhere" is a line in a letter from

    a. Karl Marx to Friedrich Engels

    b. Tom Hayden to the SDS membership

    c. James Meredith to Lyndon Johnson

    d. Martin Luther King, Jr., to his fellow clergymen

31. The slogan of Cesar Chavez's United Farm Workers in the late 1960s was

    a. "¡Viva la huelga!"

    b. "El pueblo unido"

    c. "Nosotros venceremos"

    d. "Sal si puedes"

32. To what did the phrase "credibility gap" originally refer?

  a. the discrepancy between speech and actions in the Nixon White House

  b. contradictory statements made by Lyndon Johnson regarding the Vietnam War

  c. the difference between actual body counts and estimated enemy casualties in Vietnam

  d. the indifference of Southern self-styled "law-abiding" citizens to civil rights laws

33. The Latin term *in loco parentis* was used in the 1960s to refer to a condition existing

  a. at the Pentagon

  b. on hippie communes

  c. in Southeast Asia

  d. on university campuses

34. Fill in the blank: "Turn on, tune in, _____"

  a. "be free"

  b. "let go"

  c. "drop out"

  d. "make love"

35. Who said, "You're either part of the solution or part of the problem"?

  a. Eldridge Cleaver

  b. John F. Kennedy

  c. Betty Friedan

  d. Ken Kesey

36. Before this figure became the symbol of the women's movement, it was

    a. a Native American symbol meaning "we speak truth"

    b. the Egyptian symbol for the planet Venus

    c. the symbol for the Amazon on the Brazilian flag

    d. part of a sculpture by Louise Nevelson

37. Which revolutionary hero is *not* matched correctly with his slogan?

    a. Mao Zedong: "Dare to struggle, dare to win."

    b. Karl Marx and Friedrich Engels: "Workers of the world, unite!"

    c. Frantz Fanon: "All land to the peasants!"

    d. Che Guevara: "Two, three . . . many Vietnams!"

38. A media phrase used to describe the lack of understanding between baby boomers and their parents was

    a. "We Are the Children"

    b. "The New Frontier"

    c. "The War at Home"

    d. "The Generation Gap"

39. Young workers for Eugene McCarthy's 1968 presidential campaign used the slogan

   a. "Peace in Our Time"

   b. "The Children's Crusade"

   c. "Stop the War"

   d. "Clean for Gene"

UPI / Bettman News Photos

40. What message are these people sending?

   a. "Ban the Bomb"

   b. "Peace"

   c. "Two More Years"

   d. "Victory in Vietnam"

TEST 9: Explanatory Answers

1. **(c)** The song "Age of Aquarius" was from the musical *Hair*, which opened in 1967. In astrology the Age of Aquarius is supposed to last from 2000 to 4000 A.D., superseding the Age of Pisces, which lasts from 0 to 2000 A.D. In the Age of Aquarius science and technology will be balanced by humanity. Supposedly, the influence of the coming astrological age can be felt at the end of the century; thus, the 1960s were seen as "the dawning of the Age of Aquarius."

2. **(b)** Abbie Hoffman described Woodstock as "the first attempt to land man on the Earth" because he saw the events at the music festival as both farfetched and miraculous—like space travel. By comparing the festival to the space program, Hoffman stressed the newness of the peaceful cooperation he saw on that upstate farm, as well as the participants' need to learn from and understand the Woodstock experience.

3. **(b)** Though Nixon made this statement privately after his election in 1968, in fact he *was* the first president to lose a war. After the invasion of Cambodia and the enormous wave of protest against it, "Vietnamization" (Nixon's plan to turn over the bulk of the fighting to the South Vietnamese) was speeded up. American troops were gradually withdrawn, and eventually the stage was set for North Vietnam's victory in 1975.

4. **(a)** The line, from which the Lower East Side Motherfuckers took their name, is from a poem by LeRoi Jones (Imamu Amiri Baraka) entitled "Black People!" from his collection *Black Art*, written in 1965-1966. Baraka is a poet and playwright who believes in black separatism.

5. **(b)** Yin (the negative) and yang (the positive) are Taoist terms that have many meanings, among them the mundane and the celestial, the acquired and the instinctive, the human mind and the mind of Tao. Taoists attempt to overcome yin and aid yang, then to blend the two, and finally to transcend them both. The symbol represents the two forces in balance.

6. **(c)** "Dump the Hump" was the slogan of antiwar activists who anticipated that the 1968 Democratic presidential nomination would go to Hubert Humphrey, the archetypal "cold war liberal"

who as vice-president had never once wavered from his staunch support for the war. Many of these activists backed Senator Eugene McCarthy as an antiwar candidate. The bitterness of the campaign against Humphrey, who did indeed win the nomination, in the final analysis probably helped Richard Nixon win the presidency.

7. **(b)** The quote is the opening to the Port Huron Statement, drafted by Tom Hayden and amended by other members of Students for a Democratic Society in Port Huron, Michigan, in 1962. The statement set forth the philosophy and aims of SDS but grew to represent the ideals of the New Left as a whole. Chief among the points made in the document is the call for a return to true participatory democracy, an important goal of the 1960s counterculture.

8. **(d)** In April 1967 authorities from San Francisco's City Hall and Department of Health responded to the huge influx of hippies to the Haight-Ashbury by issuing warnings and closing businesses on Haight Street for violations ranging from overcrowding to lack of doors. In protest, hippies marched down Haight Street chanting, "Haight is love." In the demonstration, over thirty people were arrested.

9. **(a)** A *bummer*, originally the word for a bad LSD trip, evolved to mean any bad experience. Early LSD experiences were rarely bad because the LSD that was then synthesized was relatively pure. However, as the making and selling of acid became a lucrative business, bummers became more common.

10. **(a)** In June 1966, Martin Luther King, Jr., Floyd McKissock, and Stokely Carmichael of the Student Nonviolent Coordinating Committee (SNCC) joined James Meredith's solitary protest march across Mississippi. After being arrested in Greenwood, Carmichael gave a speech in which he stated, "We want black power." King protested, urging the crowd to chant "freedom now!" but "black power" was the cry of the hour and became the slogan not only of later civil rights efforts but also of the Black Panthers. The slogan is sometimes attributed to another SNCC member, Willie Ricks.

11. **(b)** As the number of American soldiers killed in combat rose to five hundred a month and as Johnson continued to ask for more troop support in Vietnam, antiwar activists held the

president accountable for the lives lost in Southeast Asia. Johnson called the chant "that horrible song," as Todd Gitlin reports in his book *The Sixties: Years of Hope, Days of Rage* (1987).

12. **(a)** In his book *Die Nigger Die!* (1969), H. Rap Brown made this statement about violence. At the time, he was chairman of SNCC. As early as 1965 Brown was advocating violence as the way to a black revolution; in 1967 he threatened to bring a bomb to the March on the Pentagon. In 1969 he was arrested for inciting a crowd to arson; he is now a Muslim and runs a health food store in Georgia.

13. **(c)** On February 7, 1968, during the Tet offensive, American troops bombed the South Vietnamese town of Ben Tre almost out of existence. Ben Tre is also known as the town where Graham Greene conceived the idea for his novel *The Quiet American*. The quote is attributed to an anonymous major.

14. **(d)** Originally, the clenched fist was the salute of European Socialists and Communists, often accompanied by the strains of the "Internationale." The Black Panthers adopted the salute, and it was brought to worldwide attention during the 1968 Olympics. Tommie Smith and Lee Evans, gold- and bronze-medal winners in the 200-meter race, raised their clenched fists during the awards ceremony and were expelled from the Olympic Village. Evans, along with Larry James and Ron Freeman, medal winners in the 400-meter race, repeated the gesture a few days later, wearing black berets and black leather gloves, as a protest against prejudice in the world of sports.

15. **(c)** The aim of Nixon's "Vietnamization" program, in which the bulk of the fighting was gradually turned over to the South Vietnamese, was a "peace with honor" that would not seem like a defeat. The phrase itself dates from an 1878 speech by Benjamin Disraeli; it was also used in 1938 by British Prime Minister Neville Chamberlain to describe the outcome of his negotiations with Hitler over the fate of Czechoslovakia.

16. **(d)** Air Force General Curtis LeMay was one of the Joint Chiefs of Staff in 1967 when American ships in the Gulf of Tonkin were reportedly attacked by the North Vietnamese. This remark, a reaction to that attack, was made on May 6, 1964.

17. **(b)** When this idea was first expressed by Senator John Jordan Crittenden of Kentucky in the 19th century, he was speaking about another war unpopular with Americans, the Mexican War. He stated, "I hope to find my country in the right; however, I will stand by her, right or wrong." In 1899 the sentiment was modified by Senator Carl Schurz of Missouri, who said, "Our country, right or wrong. When right, to be kept right; when wrong, to be put right." This latter idea was discarded by those supporters of America's involvement in Vietnam who considered antiwar protests to be anti-American.

18. **(c)** The ohm symbol is used in physics to represent the unit of measure of electrical resistance. The symbol was adopted by the Stop the Draft Committee to symbolize resistance to the draft.

19. **(a)** James Brown's 1965 hit record, "Say It Loud, I'm Black and I'm Proud," echoed the growing feeling among black people of pride in their heritage. Brown had great influence on blacks in the 1960s; his success as a musician gave him the freedom to sponsor programs for poor children and to invest in black-owned businesses. After the assassination of Martin Luther King, Jr., in 1968, Brown spoke on national television to ease racial tensions between blacks and whites.

20. **(c)** In 1966 the new governor of California, Ronald Reagan, described the growing number of hippies in San Francisco in this uncomplimentary way. Reagan's attitude toward the youth of the counterculture was more clearly shown in his response to the 1969 People's Park demonstrations in Berkeley: he ordered the National Guard into the city, where they tear-gassed the protesters. In 1970 he acknowledged the possibility of a necessary "bloodbath" to put down campus unrest; he was on the Weathermen's list of enemies, along with Chicago Mayor Richard Daley, Richard Nixon, and Lyndon Johnson.

21. **(a)** As television cameras recorded the melee on the streets of Chicago during the Democratic convention of 1968, the crowd began to chant, "The whole world is watching!"

22. **(b)** The phrase, with its militant overtones, was coined by a Los Angeles disc jockey and was associated with the Black Power movement and particularly with arson during the 1965 uprising in the Watts ghetto of Los Angeles. It was probably repeated more by the media than by people actually involved in ghetto disturbances. Mayor Richard Daley of Chicago was among many who called for the shooting on sight of arsonists.

23. **(c)** The mantra most famous in the West is the Sanskrit word *om*, meant to be chanted while the worshipper is in deep contemplation of the ultimate reality. The Grateful Dead hosted an Om Festival during the Summer of Love, in which 2,500 people listened to music and chanted *om* together.

24. **(d)** Inscribed on T-shirts and bumper stickers, this aphorism said as much about the state of sexual relations at the time as it did about antiwar sentiment.

25. **(c)** Methamphetamine, often called speed, is a stimulant often used to treat obesity. By 1967 many residents of the Haight-Ashbury had turned from acid to speed, usually the potent crystal Methedrine, injected into the bloodstream. Speed freaks relied on barbiturates or heroin to bring them down from speed highs. Some developed paranoid delusions from lack of sleep, and many became violent. Speed overdoses were not uncommon.

26. **(c)** Allen Ginsberg used the phrase at a Berkeley rally in 1965, and "flower power" became the hippies' antiwar theme. The flower theme appeared in songs—"Where Have All the Flowers Gone?" and "San Francisco (Be Sure to Wear Flowers in Your Hair)"—and in fashion. The photograph (page 58) of the hippie inserting flowers in the barrel of a gun is a famous reflection of this peaceful sentiment. The term "flower children" was often used by the media to refer to the hippies.

27. **(a)** One of many chants popular in antiwar marches of the Vietnam era, this one rather prophetically refers to the defeat of the South by the North Vietnamese under Ho Chi Minh and by National Liberation Front forces.

28. **(a)** Newton credited the Black Panthers with coining this phrase, which paraphrases Lenin. Its call for empowerment could also apply to Saul Alinsky and his Industrial Areas Foundation, which worked to organize urban neighborhoods; to Cesar Chavez and his United Farm Workers; to SDS and its organizing projects among the urban poor; and to SNCC and CORE and their battle for voting rights.

29. **(c)** The British Campaign for Nuclear Disarmament adopted this symbol in 1958. According to Elisabeth Helfman's book *Signs and Symbols Around the World* (1967), it combines the semaphore symbols for letters *N* and *D* within a circle representing the unborn child. The combination of semaphore letters makes an upside-down version of the ancient symbol for man. Thus, the whole sign stands for the death of man and the unborn child. It became more universally recognized as a symbol for peace in the mid-1960s.

30. **(d)** King's "Letter from a Birmingham Jail," written after one of his many arrests, was a response to an open letter from local clergymen who objected to his activist tactics. The letter is dated April 16, 1963, but it was published nationwide for the first time in the August 1963 edition of the *Atlantic Monthly.*

31. **(a)** "Long live the strike" was the chant of UFW members as they carried on successful strikes and boycotts against lettuce and grape growers. Chavez's organization included blacks, whites, and Filipinos as well as Mexican-Americans.

32. **(b)** Later popularized by Murrey Marder and others at the *Washington Post,* the phrase appeared originally in a piece by David Wise in the *New York Herald Tribune* in May 1965. Wise used the term in describing a speech by Johnson in which the president declared that although we need guns and bombs, they are nonetheless "witnesses to human folly." "Credibility gap" thus referred to a lack of believability created when official statements contradict each other.

33. **(d)** *In loco parentis,* or "in place of a parent," referred to the general attitude and policy of universities and colleges toward students as the decade began. As students sought empowerment in the social and academic arenas of college life, they challenged this concept. A common argument was that if students were old enough to be sent to war, they were adult enough to do without a curfew, choose their own curricula, and so on. Richard Fariña's novel *Been Down So Long It Looks Like Up to Me* (1966) centers around a battle over *in loco parentis* at a thinly disguised Cornell University. The concept has recently turned up again on campuses such as Boston University as colleges attempt to redefine their roles and reassert control.

34. **(c)** Timothy Leary summed up his philosophy with this phrase, which was also the title of a lecture he gave around the country beginning in 1967. Listeners were advised to "turn on [to the scene], tune in [to what is happening], and drop out [of high school, college, grad school . . .]."

35. **(a)** Cleaver probably said this in 1968. Its sentiment is similar to Kesey's "Now, you're either on the bus or off the bus" (in Wolfe's *Electric Kool-Aid Acid Test*) and Christ's "He that is not with me is against me" (Matthew 12:30).

36. **(b)** Symbols for the planets were used both in astrology and astronomy. Egyptian astronomers created an entire solar system alphabet in which the symbol for Venus resembled the goddess's handmirror and the one for Mars represented a spear and shield. The symbols later took on more general meanings of female and male in botany and other areas of biology.

37. **(c)** This was one of the slogans of the Bolshevik party under Lenin. Frantz Fanon (1925–1961), a Martiniquan, was a hero of the Algerian revolution and a revolutionary theorist of great influence. Mao's "Dare to struggle . . ." became an antiwar chant as the movement became more radical. It celebrated revolutionary struggle instead of the pacifists' gentler themes. Che's call for "two, three . . . many Vietnams" was controversial even among his followers, who, Che said, regretted "the blood spilled and that to be spilled in case of three or four Vietnams."

38. **(d)** The noted anthropologist Margaret Mead probably summed up the situation best in *Culture and Commitment* (1970): "Even very recently, the elders could say: 'You know I have been young and you have never been old.' But today's young people can reply: 'You have never been young in the world I am young in, and you never can be . . .' This break between generations is wholly new: it is planetary and universal."

39. **(d)** In a last attempt to work within the system, hundreds of young students attracted to McCarthy's antiwar theme and avuncular presence cut their hair and dressed "Establishment" to go door-to-door in New Hampshire before the primary and get out the vote. The results proved the power of this "Clean for Gene" campaign: McCarthy got 42.4 percent of the vote to Johnson's 49.5, a remarkable showing against an incumbent president.

40. **(b)** It is difficult to know just when the "V for Victory" sign beloved by Churchill and Nixon took on the connotation of "Victory for the Peace Movement," but in their 1978 *Woodstock Census*, Rex Weiner and Deanne Stillman gleefully report that 81 percent of their respondents "flashed [the sign] to perfect strangers" during the antiwar era.

Steal This Book: Literature

Writers are always selling someone out.

—*JOAN DIDION*

---

1. A 1970 book by Charles Reich that analyzed the countercultural movement in terms of a change in consciousness was titled
   a. *The Sexual Revolution*
   b. *The Greening of America*
   c. *The Rebel*
   d. *Beyond Culture*

2. Which of these books are by the novelist and Merry Prankster leader Ken Kesey?
   a. *The Kandy-Kolored Tangerine-Flake Streamline Baby* and *The Electric Kool-Aid Acid Test*
   b. *The Dharma Bums* and *Satori in Paris*
   c. *One Flew Over the Cuckoo's Nest* and *Sometimes a Great Notion*
   d. *A Coney Island of the Mind* and *An Eye on the World*

3. Eldridge Cleaver wrote most of *Soul on Ice* (1968) while
   a. in exile in Algeria
   b. serving as minister of information for the Black Panther party
   c. working for *Ramparts* magazine
   d. in Folsom Prison

4. The writers Jack Gelber and Arthur Kopit achieved fame in the 1960s for their
   a. poetry
   b. plays
   c. political essays
   d. novels

5. What did the Latin American-born author Carlos Castaneda contribute to the counterculture?
   a. books exploring age-old Mexican Indian rituals
   b. a widely read translation of the speeches of Fidel Castro

   c. a day-by-day account of the United Farm Workers' strike in California

   d. a novel based on the exploits of the Puerto Rican Young Lord activists in New York City

6. What was the title of Jerry Rubin's 1970 book about rock music, television, and revolution?

   a. *Do it!*

   b. *Be Here Now*

   c. *Ringolevio*

   d. *Vietnam*

7. Nikki Giovanni's late-1960s poetry dealt with themes of

   a. lesbianism and gay rights

   b. revolution and racism

   c. communal living and societal dropouts

   d. drugs and spiritualism

8. Before achieving fame with the novel *Roots*, Alex Haley collaborated on a widely read 1965 book entitled

   a. *Jubilee*

   b. *White Man, Listen!*

   c. *The Autobiography of Malcolm X*

   d. *Airport*

9. Richard Fariña, who met an untimely death in 1966, was a novelist and well-known

   a. folksinger

   b. civil rights activist

   c. United Farm Workers organizer

   d. poster artist

10. What did readers find in Mao Zedong's "little red book"?

   a. essays on communism by everyone from Lenin to Ch'en Tu-hsiu

b. poems in accepted revolutionary style

c. an interview with the American correspondent Anna Louise Strong

d. quotations from the Chairman on a variety of subjects

11. Joseph Heller's first novel was a hit with the counter-culture because of its focus on

    a. the numbing boredom of corporate life

    b. the absurdity of war and the blind exercise of official power

    c. the human need for self-expression

    d. the repressive nature of suburban existence

12. The writer Tom Wolfe became famous in the 1960s for his tradition-breaking

    a. "New Journalism"

    b. plays and novels about the New South

    c. picaresque fiction

    d. science fiction trilogies

13. The absurdist works of the French playwright Jean Genet became popular in the 1960s for their depiction of

    a. oppression and thwarted revolt

    b. love and the power of faith

    c. the strength of youth and the frailty of the ego

    d. the banality of middle-class life

14. Which of the following playwrights wrote *Viet Rock* and *Approaching Simone?*

    a. Maria Irene Fornes

    b. Terrence McNally

    c. Megan Terry

    d. Jules Feiffer

15. What happens in the 1964 play *Dutchman* by LeRoi Jones (Imamu Amiri Baraka)?

   a. A white woman seduces, enrages, and kills a black man.

   b. A ghetto child, killed accidentally, is resurrected.

   c. Workers on a chain gang escape and make their way to Atlanta.

   d. A black uprising in South Africa is quashed by the Boers.

16. Why was the 1928 book *Lady Chatterley's Lover* important in the 1960s?

   a. Its mystical style was imitated by avant-garde hippie poets.

   b. It was the subject of a legal case that broke the barriers of censorship.

   c. It was the earliest precursor of the decade's feminist fiction.

   d. It was the first novel to employ stream-of-consciousness.

17. What did the poets Anne Sexton, John Berryman, and Sylvia Plath have in common?

   a. All three committed suicide.

   b. All three wrote in the "confessional" tradition.

   c. All three won the Pulitzer Prize.

   d. all of the above

18. A major influence on the 1960s short stories of Donald Barthelme was

   a. space travel

   b. the civil rights movement

   c. television

   d. Southeast Asian culture

19. A diary published in the radical magazine *Ramparts* in July 1968 found its audience among

   a. unhappy housewives

   b. aspiring guerrilla revolutionaries

   c. civil libertarians

   d. backers of Eugene McCarthy's presidential campaign

20. Hallucinatory imagery and the recurrent theme of drug addiction mark the literary work of

   a. Gilbert Sorrentino

   b. Jerzy Kosinski

   c. William Gass

   d. William S. Burroughs

21. Why did Kahlil Gibran's *Prophet* became a 1960s cult classic?

   a. It was a biography of the Maharishi Mahesh Yogi.

   b. It was an account of life in a Tibetan monastery.

   c. It spoke of the promise of redemption through love.

   d. It showed how astrology could be used to save the world.

22. Which of the following writers became famous for chronicling both the doings of the Hell's Angels and the 1972 presidential campaign?

   a. Hunter S. Thompson

   b. Thomas Pynchon

   c. Norman Mailer

   d. Tom Wolfe

23. Which of the following authors wrote *Steal This Book* and *Soon to Be a Major Motion Picture?*

   a. Todd Gitlin

   b. Abbie Hoffman

   c. Jerry Rubin

   d. Tom Hayden

24. Richard Brautigan's popular works of offbeat fiction included

   a. *Reflections on a Gift of Watermelon Pickle*

   b. *Manchild in the Promised Land* and *The Children of Ham*

   c. *Big as Life* and *The Book of Daniel*

   d. *Trout Fishing in America* and *In Watermelon Sugar*

25. Which of the following authors wrote popular novels describing an icy end to the world and a character kidnapped by aliens?

   a. Kurt Vonnegut

   b. George Orwell

   c. Aldous Huxley

   d. Elia Kazan

26. Who was Frodo?

   a. the founder of a Southern California literary movement based on transcendental meditation

   b. a Haight-Ashbury poet and draft resister who wrote under the influence of LSD

   c. a character in J. R. R. Tolkien's *Lord of the Rings*

   d. the imaginary priest/narrator of a poem by Kahlil Gibran

27. Which of the following are sensitive portrayals of black personal and family life by the writer Lorraine Hansberry?

   a. *The Small Room* and *Kinds of Love*

   b. *Living in America* and *Reversals*

   c. *A Raisin in the Sun* and *To Be Young, Gifted and Black*

   d. *A Man and Two Women* and *African Stories*

28. Which of these musicians did *not* write a book?

   a. Bob Dylan

   b. John Lennon

   c. Leonard Cohen

   d. Jerry Garcia

29. What made the *Tibetan Book of the Dead* popular among 1960s hippies?

   a. It gives instructions on how to live in harmony with the world.

   b. Its descriptions of dying are similar to LSD hallucinations.

   c. It celebrates the virtues of communal living and free love.

   d. It explains how to overcome the fear of death through meditation.

30. The critic Susan Sontag, in her 1966 book *Against Interpretation,* argued that

   a. any work of fiction can be interpreted in one of five ways

   b. audiences should respond to a creative work emotionally, not intellectually

   c. art is a more important medium than literature

   d. modern fiction cannot be interpreted

31. In *The Fire Next Time* (1963), the great black writer James Baldwin called for

   a. a spirit of love between blacks and whites

   b. a violent black revolution

   c. strict separation of the races

   d. a return to Africa for black Americans

32. What happens in the classic Hindu epic called the *Ramayana?*

   a. Two royal families struggle for the throne.

   b. Krishna and a warrior discuss the meaning of life.

   c. A prince wins his bride from a demon-king.

   d. The stories of Vishnu's various incarnations are related.

33. In a 1922 German novel much admired by 1960s hippies, who was Siddhartha?

   a. Muhammad

   b. Buddha

   c. Jesus

   d. Brahma

34. The author David Halberstam spent the early 1960s

   a. as a journalist writing opinionated reports on the war in Vietnam

   b. writing novels based on the real-life adventures of counterculture figures

   c. creating poetry that blended drug and nature imagery

   d. writing magazine reviews of early countercultural experiments in art and theater

35. Which of the following writers produced a widely read volume of essays on the counterculture and life in California?

   a. Grace Paley

   b. Maxine Kumin

   c. Joan Didion

   d. Alice Munro

36. What was the subject of Norman Mailer's 1968 book *Armies of the Night?*

   a. an attack on Da Nang during the Vietnam War

b. the October 1967 March on the Pentagon

c. demonstrators who blocked troop trains in California

d. Black Panther rallies in 1966 in Oakland, California

37. A poet whose 1960s work reflected American Indian and Zen Buddhist philosophies is

    a. Ama Ata Aidoo

    b. May Swenson

    c. Gary Snyder

    d. A. R. Ammons

38. Which of the following novels is a 1960s allegory of 20th-century intellectual despair, set at a mythical university?

    a. *Goodbye, Columbus*

    b. *Snow White*

    c. *Vital Parts*

    d. *Giles Goat-Boy*

39. The *Kama-sutra*, a Hindu book popular with the counterculture, is

    a. the epic tale of a goddess's love for a mortal

    b. the life story of the god Kama

    c. a chronicle of the lives of Indian holy men

    d. a description of Indian lovemaking techniques

40. What was so shocking about the future in the 1970 book *Future Shock?*

    a. the threat of nuclear holocaust

    b. the technological and social changes to which people would be subjected

    c. the all-but-certain creation of a totalitarian state

    d. the use of eugenics to breed "perfect" humans

TEST 10: *Explanatory Answers*

1. **(b)** *The Greening of America* appeared in excerpts in the *New Yorker* in September 1970, and the book rapidly became a best-seller. The author was Charles Reich, a Yale law professor who argued that the sixties counterculture signaled a change in human perception of reality, a change he called "Consciousness III." Whereas Consciousness I had been the pioneer spirit that built America and Consciousness II was the organized mindset of corporate America, Consciousness III heralded a utopian state in which the corporate superstructure would be dismantled. Reich received extensive media attention for his celebration of the hippie lifestyle, but events in the early 1970s plainly indicated that Consciousness III was only transitory. The other books listed are by Wilhelm Reich, Albert Camus, and Lionel Trilling.

2. **(c)** Ken Kesey is better known as the protagonist of Tom Wolfe's *Electric Kool-Aid Acid Test* than for his own fiction. *One Flew Over the Cuckoo's Nest* (1962) is set in a mental institution. The hero tries to inspire the inmates to assert control over the head nurse, with terrifying results. The novel was the basis for a play and later (1975) an award-winning film. *Sometimes a Great Notion* (1964) is the story of a family of loggers in Oregon. It too was turned into a moderately successful film (1971). Kesey headed the Merry Pranksters, a band of California acidheads and hippies, throughout much of the decade, and it is this part of his life that Tom Wolfe describes. The other works listed are by Wolfe, Jack Kerouac, and Lawrence Ferlinghetti.

3. **(d)** Cleaver was serving a prison sentence for rape when he began writing *Soul on Ice*, his first book. His lawyer sent portions to *Ramparts* editor-in-chief Edward Keating, who offered encouragement. By the time Cleaver was paroled in 1966, the manuscript was nearly finished. *Soul on Ice* analyzes the interrelationships among black men, black women, white men, and white women and explores self-hatred in women and blacks. Cleaver later became an editor at *Ramparts* and joined the Black Panthers, soon becoming minister of information. In 1968 he was the California Peace and Freedom party's candidate for president of the United States. His Panther activities brought constant surveillance by police, and

he was arrested for violating his parole. Instead of returning to prison, he fled underground, traveling first to Cuba and later to Algeria. In 1975 he returned to the United States and gave himself up. Cleaver is now a born-again Christian and is involved in politics as a conservative Republican.

4. **(b)** *The Connection* (1959) by Jack Gelber was the most famous early production of the Living Theatre. Its characters include four heroin addicts, the "producer" of the play, the "author" of the play, four jazz musicians, and two "photographers" who are "filming" the piece. Actors range up the aisles of the theater and into the lobby, challenging audience members to face their own addictions. Gelber followed this work with other pieces for the Living Theatre that looked at social and artistic issues; *The Apple* (1961) and *The Cuban Thing* (1968) are two of several plays written in the 1960s. Arthur Kopit's first successful work was the absurdist *Oh Dad Poor Dad Mama's Hung You in the Closet and I'm Feeling So Sad* (1962), but perhaps more important is *Indians* (1968). Using the motif of Buffalo Bill's Wild West Show, Kopit explored the ways that oppressors create myths to justify their oppression. The parallel with Vietnam was clear.

5. **(a)** Castaneda was born in Peru but immigrated to the United States and trained as an anthropologist. In books titled *The Teaching of Don Juan* (1968), *A Separate Reality* (1971), and *Journey to Ixtlan* (1972), he documented the apprentice-ship of the graduate student Carlos to the sorcerer Don Juan Matus. The old Indian shows Carlos the path to religious experience through natural hallucinogens and physical exer-cise. Whether the books are true anthropology or fiction, they were widely read by those interested in mind expansion.

6. **(a)** One of the original Yippies, Rubin gained fame with the 1967 March on the Pentagon and went on to be a co-defendant in the trial of the Chicago Seven. While awaiting trial, he penned this rambling work, subtitled *Scenarios of the Revo-lution*, in which he discussed rock music, the role of television in revolution, revolution as theater, and the virtue of dropping out of school. The book was published in 1970 with an introduction by Eldridge Cleaver. Today Rubin runs "net-working parties" for young Manhattan executives. The other books listed are by Baba Ram Dass (Richard Alpert), Emmett Grogan, and Mary McCarthy.

7. **(b)** The majority of Giovanni's work is political and deals with issues of black poverty, racism, and revolution. *Black Feeling, Black Talk* (1969) contains poems dedicated to H. Rap Brown and the Black Panthers. *Black Judgment* (1969) features "The Funeral of Martin Luther King, Jr.," and "Nikki-Rosa," an often-anthologized rejection of the notion that a poor childhood is an unhappy one.

8. **(c)** *The Autobiography of Malcolm X* (1965) was published just as Malcolm himself was murdered, and it became a bible of the Black Power movement. Chapter 1 opens with the Ku Klux Klan sweeping down on the home of Malcolm's family— his father had been an organizer for Marcus Garvey's back-to-Africa movement—and traces the dissolution of the family after his father's murder and his mother's nervous breakdown. The book continues into Malcolm's adulthood, up to his Muslim conversion. The other books listed are by Margaret Walker, Richard Wright, and Arthur Hailey.

9. **(a)** With his wife Mimi, sister of Joan Baez, Richard Fariña (1937–1966) toured the coffeehouse circuit and recorded three albums of folk music. He also wrote articles and plays while awaiting the publication of the novel he began in the late 1950s, *Been Down So Long It Looks Like Up to Me* (1966). The novel, set on the campus of Mentor (Cornell) University, chronicles the adventures of Gnossos Pappadopoulis as he faces curfews for coeds, an influx of new and potent drugs, and the changing of the guard between the beats and the new standard-bearers of the counterculture. Fariña was killed in a motorcycle accident following a publication party for the book. He was twenty-nine.

10. **(d)** Mao Zedong did most of his writing in 1935–1945 in the mountains of northwestern China, where he and his Communist followers had sought refuge following the Long March. In 1959, after Mao had been in power for ten years, Lin Biao became minister of defense and vowed to make the People's Liberation Army into a "great school of Mao Zedong's thought." That year the army published *Quotations from Chairman Mao*, a varied collection of pithy sayings and writings running the gamut from Mao's early articles on the rights of women to his tomes on guerrilla warfare. The book was translated into dozens of languages, glorified in Chinese art of the 1960s, and

widely circulated among New Leftists in the American counterculture.

11. **(b)** *Catch-22* (1961) tells the story of Yossarian, a bomber pilot in World War II who dreams of nothing but finishing his tour and going home. With every mission he flies, however, his commanders add more missions to his quota. Yossarian refuses to fly anymore and pleads insanity, but the camp doctor tells him about "catch-22": "If he flew them he was crazy and didn't have to; but if he didn't want to he was sane and had to." This neat summation of bureaucratic power run amok captured the fancy of a nation embroiled in a catch-22 conflict in Vietnam. Mike Nichols directed a film adaptation of the novel in 1970.

12. **(a)** "New Journalism" refers to a writing style typified by Tom Wolfe, in which the journalist is an active voice rather than a mere recording device. As narrator of a piece, the New Journalist feels free to comment, analyze, describe, digress—anything to paint a clear picture for the reader. An astute observer of American pop culture, Wolfe has reported on everything from the space program to cocktail parties benefiting the Black Panthers. Collections of his essays published in the 1960s include *The Kandy-Kolored Tangerine-Flake Streamline Baby* (1965) and *The Pump-House Gang* (1968). *The Electric Kool-Aid Acid Test* (1968) chronicles the adventures of Ken Kesey and his Merry Pranksters as they ride their Magic Bus across the country.

13. **(a)** The plays of Jean Genet (1910–1986) merged Artaud's Theatre of Cruelty with the Theatre of the Absurd. Genet's most important plays deal with repressed people trying unsuccessfully to change their lives. Because of his own background—thief, prostitute, pimp—Genet had a fascination with the underworld that he transferred to his dramas. In *The Maids* (1948, translated 1954), two servants poison their mistress's tea, but when she leaves without drinking, one maid drinks it herself. *The Balcony* (1957, translated 1960) features a brothel where the male customers act out their fantasies, only to find that their dreams-come-true are nightmares—the revolutionary, for example, discovers that the tyranny he wants to overthrow is really the tyranny he hopes to impose on others. *The Blacks* (1959, translated 1960) centers on a confrontation between the black cast and the

white audience members, with the ironic twist that the confrontation can take place only when the blacks are playing a role. *The Screens* (1961, translated 1962) is based in part on the Algerian conflict.

14. **(c)** Megan Terry and Jean-Claude van Itallie were the primary playwrights for the Open Theatre, and the collective improvisatory techniques used by that troupe are reflected in their work. *Viet Rock* (1966) is a rock musical about the war. *Approaching Simone* (1970) is a paean to the French Catholic philosopher Simone Weil, whose writings dealt with moral issues of pacifism, oppression, and freedom.

15. **(a)** A painful tale of racial hatred, *Dutchman* (1964) takes place on a subway careening endlessly underground (like the mythical ship the *Flying Dutchman*). Lula, a white woman, addresses a black man named Clay. She begins seductively but slowly becomes caustic, making fun of his "white" behavior and values. Clay, furious, admits that his manner is all fakery; all blacks mask their hatred toward all whites. Hearing this, Lula stabs Clay and has the passengers throw his body off the train. As the play ends, another black man enters the subway car.

16. **(b)** The novel by D. H. Lawrence (1885–1930) contains explicit sexual passages, and it was banned as obscene until 1959 in the United States (and until 1960 in England). The court case that led to the lifting of the ban set important precedents for obscenity law and established an atmosphere of openness not seen before. The significance of the ruling for 1960s writers was great; many publications of the time might otherwise have been censored.

17. **(d)** The "confessional" school of poets includes W. D. Snodgrass and Robert Lowell as well as Sexton (1928–1974), Berryman (1914–1972), and Plath (1932–1963). Marked by introspection and angst, the work of these poets influenced the next generation of writers. Sexton won the Pulitzer Prize for *Live or Die* (1966) and continued a personal infatuation with death through *The Death Notebooks* (1974) before killing herself. Berryman won the prize for *77 Dream Songs* (1964) and continued to write poems about his struggle with alcohol and despair until his suicide. *Ariel* (1965), a collection of poems written just before Plath's suicide, contains terrifying imagery

from the postwar world. Plath gained even more attention with her single novel, *The Bell Jar* (1963). Published first under a pseudonym, it appeared under her name only in 1971, by which time it was a favorite on campuses across the country. The heroine, clearly Plath herself, is plagued by mental illness and the urge to end her life. Plath won a posthumous Pulitzer in 1982 for her collected poems. She and Sexton were among the first to write about what it meant to be a woman in the postwar era; they described the personal, internal struggle of women in America, a theme that would later be picked up and politicized in the women's movement.

18. **(c)** *Benét's Readers Encyclopedia* calls Barthelme's short fiction "the verbal equivalents of pop art," referring to the sound-bite-like elements of his disjointed writing. Barthelme (1931–1989) is best known for short stories such as those included in *Come Back, Dr. Caligari* (1964) and *Unspeakable Practices, Unnatural Acts* (1968). Sprinkled throughout his comic prose are advertising slogans, references to television shows and movies, and other reflections of pop culture.

19. **(b)** *The Diary of Che Guevara* chronicles that guerrilla leader's exploits in Bolivia from November 7, 1966, until his capture in October 1967. It contains musings on revolution as well as a record of the grueling day-to-day life of a guerrilla band. The diary was made public by Che's Cuban comrades and was published in English by *Ramparts* with an introduction by Fidel Castro.

20. **(d)** An inspiration to the beats, William S. Burroughs used his own heroin addiction as a motif in *Naked Lunch* (1959) and *Junkie* (1964). His prose in these and other novels is disjointed, seemingly random, with the effect of a hallucination. *The Wild Boys* (1971), about homosexual hashish smokers, has a more traditional narrative structure. Burroughs is as notorious for his own exploits as for his works; besides his forays into drugs and the seamy underworld of Morocco, he is remembered for accidentally killing his wife during a foolish pistol-target game.

21. **(c)** Kahlil Gibran (1883–1931) was a Syrian who immigrated to America at the turn of the century. He is the author of novels, prose poems, and plays, many of which treat human problems in a mystical way. *The Prophet* (1923), a prose poem, was translated into thirteen languages and enjoyed a new popularity in the 1960s, when its message of love appealed to the counterculture.

22. **(a)** Hunter S. Thompson began his journalism career working for the *New York Herald Tribune* and the *National Observer* in the early 1960s. In 1965 he moved to San Francisco, where he shared an apartment with members of the Hell's Angels motorcycle gang. He wrote an article on the Angels for *The Nation*, which he later expanded into a book entitled *Hell's Angels*. As the book became a success, Thompson met Ken Kesey and Tom Wolfe, introducing them to each other and to the Angels, to whom Kesey gave LSD. After the Angels book, Thompson went on to write *Fear and Loathing in Las Vegas* (1971) and *Fear and Loathing on the Campaign Trail* (1972), both pointed political and/or social commentaries. Thompson's alter-ego, Raoul Duke, who is both a fictional character and a personification of 1960s values, has been immortalized in Gary Trudeau's comic strip *Doonesbury*.

23. **(b)** Erstwhile Yippie Abbie Hoffman wrote his first book, *Revolution for the Hell of It*, in 1968. By giving his later works titles such as *Steal This Book* (1971), Hoffman was trying to make his writings as subversive as his other activities. Most of his works gave instructions and advice on how to live in the counterculture. *Soon to Be a Major Motion Picture* (1980) is Hoffman's description of his life during the 1960s.

24. **(d)** Richard Brautigan (1933–1984) achieved prominence in the 1960s because of his offbeat fiction, which mixed elements of dreams, prose poetry, and the novel. His best-known fiction works are *Trout Fishing in America* (1967) and *In Watermelon Sugar* (1968), and he was also the author of several collections of poetry, including *The Pill Versus the Springhill Mine Disaster* (1968). The other works mentioned are a collection of poetry edited by Stephen Dunning and novels by Claude Brown and E. L. Doctorow.

25. **(a)** Vonnegut's 1963 novel *Cat's Cradle* tells of the end of the world brought about by a product that freezes everything it touches. His best-known novel, *Slaughterhouse-Five* (1969), is the story of Billy Pilgrim, a survivor of the Dresden firestorm, who is kidnapped by aliens and forced to mate with a movie star. Vonnegut was popular with the counterculture because

of his darkly comic style and because of their shared concerns: the world's end and the horror of war.

26. **(c)** Frodo was a hobbit, a race of beings in a series of books written by J. R. R. Tolkien (1892–1973). In the books, Frodo dwells in the mythical land of Middle Earth and gains control over a powerful ring that could bring great evil to his world. *Lord of the Rings* (1954–1956) became a cult classic in the 1960s and was seen by many as an allegory of the antagonism between the U.S. government and anti-Establishment forces. Parallels were also drawn between the power of the ring and the power of the atom.

27. **(c)** Lorraine Hansberry (1930–1965) is best known for her play *A Raisin in the Sun*, which, though it was written in 1959, addressed issues of the 1960s in its story of a black family attempting to escape the ghetto. The play won the New York Drama Critics Award. After Hansberry's death, a collection of her writings titled *To Be Young, Gifted and Black* (1969) was published and dramatized; it ran off-Broadway. Hansberry tried to dispel preconceptions about race and sex in her essays and plays; both her portrayal of the African-American identity and her treatment of women's issues were ahead of her time. The other works listed are by May Sarton, Anne Stevenson, and Doris Lessing.

28. **(d)** Bob Dylan is the author of *Tarantula* (1970), a collection of writings from the 1960s. John Lennon's books *In His Own Write* (1964) and *A Spaniard in the Works* (1965) found an enthusiastic audience; they were a combination of art and writing that reflected Lennon's wit and imagination. Leonard Cohen was known as a beat poet and novelist before he turned to folk rock in the 1960s; his books include *Let Us Compare Mythologies* (1956) and *Beautiful Losers* (1966).

29. **(b)** The *Tibetan Book of the Dead* is a description of the forty-nine days that Tibetans believe a dying soul must spend in a state between life and death. The descriptions of the soul's experiences in this state are similar to the visions seen by LSD users.

30. **(b)** In *Against Interpretation* Sontag declared that the proper way to respond to a creative work is through the senses and the emotions rather than the intellect. Sontag also broke new ground in the 1960s with her book on North Vietnam, *Trip to Hanoi* (1968), and her discussion of the development of political consciousness, titled *Styles of Radical Will* (1969). Her willingness to analyze popular phenomena—pornography, science fiction, Happenings—offended conservative critics but appealed to the counterculture.

31. **(a)** Baldwin (1924–1987) expressed a fierce anger at racial prejudice in his novels and essays, but *The Fire Next Time* (1963) is not a mere polemic against white bigotry. Instead, it urges blacks to reject Muslim separatism, to go beyond their traditional church teachings, and to embrace a truly Christian spirit of love that would transcend race.

32. **(c)** The *Ramayana* (c. 500 B.C.) is the story of Rama, a prince who is the seventh incarnation of Vishnu. It is considered one of the great Indian epics and has 24,000 stanzas. In the epic, Rama's bride, Sita, is carried off at the same time that Rama is exiled from his kingdom. After Sita is rescued, Rama regains his kingdom; but Sita is then exiled because Rama fears she has been defiled. Eventually, however, the lovers are reunited. Interest in the *Ramayana* reflected the 1960s obsession with things Indian, including the works whose plots are mentioned: the *Mahabharata*, the *Bhagavadgita*, and the *Vishnu Puranas*.

33. **(b)** Herman Hesse's novel *Siddhartha* (1922) tells the story of Siddhartha Gautama (563–483 B.C.), who was given the title of Buddha and who founded the Buddhist religion. The novel is not an account of Buddha's life but the story of a nobleman whose efforts toward enlightenment parallel Buddha's. The Buddhist religion, and the novel, found enthusiastic followers in the 1960s counterculture. Other novels by Hesse (1877–1962), such as *Demian* (1919), *Steppenwolf* (1927), and *Narcissus and Goldmund* (1930) were also revived at this time and appealed to readers because of their common theme of the quest for the spiritual life.

34. **(a)** In 1962, David Halberstam, then with *The New York Times*, went to Vietnam and began reporting on what he saw there. Since the United States was not officially at war, there was little effort to censor his reports, and Halberstam's frank, opinionated accounts won him both censure and acclaim. President Kennedy tried to have him stopped from reporting,

and Madame Nhu (the sister of Vietnam's President Ngo Dinh Diem) accused him of being a Communist spy. In 1964 he was awarded a Pulitzer Prize. In 1965 he published *The Making of a Quagmire*, a report on the war; soon afterward, he returned to America, where he became an editor of *Harper's*. In 1969, Halberstam published *The Best and the Brightest*, an incisive analysis of the war and the government officials who got the United States involved in it; the book won him a large popular audience.

35. **(c)** Joan Didion's first book of essays, *Slouching towards Bethlehem* (1968), focused on the 1960s counterculture and life in California. She has also written several novels: *Run River* (1963) and *Play It As It Lays* (1970) treat the plight of modern woman in a chaotic society. Didion's political interests continue to the present: *Salvador* (1983) is a report on the guerrilla conflict in El Salvador; *Miami* (1987) describes the Cuban exile community in Florida.

36. **(b)** Mailer's history/novel, published in 1968, is a first-person account of the 1967 March on the Pentagon. The book won both the Pulitzer Prize and the National Book Award. Mailer's role as a social and political critic is evident in his collections of essays, among which are *The Presidential Papers* (1963) and *Why Are We in Vietnam?* (1967); in 1969 his politics led him to run for mayor of New York City. Mailer has had a strong impact on journalism: he helped found *The Village Voice*, edited *Dissent* magazine, and together with writers like Hunter S. Thompson and Tom Wolfe introduced the narrative style called New Journalism.

37. **(c)** Although he started as a member of the San Francisco beats and was immortalized in Jack Kerouac's *Dharma Bums*, Gary Snyder was also important to the 1960s counterculture. In the early years of the decade he spent time in a Zen Buddhist monastery, and his 1960s poetry, including *The Back Country* (1967) and *Earth House Hold* (1969), clearly shows Zen influence. Snyder has also been influenced by the culture of American Indians.

38. **(d)** Although John Barth's *Sotweed Factor* (1960) was received with great acclaim, its parody of the picaresque novel did not have as much impact on the counterculture as did *Giles Goat-Boy* (1966). Set at a monstrous university that is divided into West Campus (mirroring the Western world) and East Campus (mirroring Communist-bloc nations), the narrative involves Giles, the Grand Tutor (a Christ figure), and the struggle toward the salvation of humankind. The novel's parodic allegories gave it a cult following in the 1960s, though critics found it inferior to Barth's other novels. The other works listed are by Philip Roth, Donald Barthelme, and Thomas Berger.

39. (d) The *Kama-sutra*, written by Vatsayana around the first century A.D., is a detailed account of the art and technique of Indian erotic love. In Hinduism, love (Kama, named after the god of love) is one of the four goals of man, the others being sacred duty, material gain, and salvation. Along with other Indian writings, the *Kama-sutra* was revived in the 1960s and aided in the spread of the sexual revolution.

40. (b) Alvin Toffler was an editor of *Fortune* magazine when he wrote an article for *Horizon* magazine using the phrase "future shock." The article described "the shattering stress and disorientation that we induce in individuals by subjecting them to too much change in too short a time." Toffler spent five years studying this phenomenon and in 1970 published *Future Shock*, a book detailing the changes of the 1960s he believed would produce this fearful state. The book discusses such challenges to the status quo as black power, throw-away products, the fractured family, hippies, and communes.

Bibliography

This bibliography lists both books that were written during the 1960s and books that were written about the 1960s. Some of them are general studies of the era; others cover specific facets of the counterculture. You can find these volumes in most public libraries and bookstores.

BOOKS OF THE ERA

Politics

Halberstam, David. *The Best and the Brightest.* New York: Random House, 1972. An analysis of the Kennedy and Johnson administrations and their role in the Vietnam War.

Johnson, Lyndon Baines. *The Vantage Point.* New York: Holt, Rinehart & Winston, 1971. The Johnson presidency as seen through the eyes of the president.

White, Theodore H. *The Making of the President: 1960.* New York: Atheneum, 1961. An analysis of the 1960 presidential campaign. See also *The Making of the President: 1964* and *The Making of the President: 1968.*

Vietnam

Halberstam, David. *The Making of a Quagmire.* New York: Random House, 1965. An in-depth look at the Vietnam War by a well-known journalist.

The Pentagon Papers. New York: New York Times Books, 1971. The hidden facts behind the Vietnam War.

Civil Rights and Liberation

Forman, James. *The Making of Black Revolutionaries.* New York: Macmillan, 1972. From the civil rights movement through the Black Panthers, by the former executive secretary of SNCC and administrator of the Black Panthers.

Friedan, Betty. *The Feminine Mystique.* New York: Dell Publishing Company, 1963. A study of the role of women in society.

Newton, Huey P. *To Die for the People*. New York: Random House, 1972. The collected writings of the revolutionary.

The Counterculture

Hoffman, Abbie. *Revolution for the Hell of It*. New York: Dial Press, 1968. A guide to anti-Establishment activities.

Jacobs, Harold, ed. *Weatherman*. Berkeley, CA: Ramparts Press, 1970. A discussion of the Weatherman group.

Reich, Charles. *The Greening of America*. New York: Random House, 1970. Analyzes the counterculture in terms of a three-step change in consciousness.

Rubin, Jerry. *Do it!* New York: Ballantine Books, 1970. Brief scenes from Rubin's experiences in the counterculture.

Thompson, Hunter S. *Hell's Angels*. New York: Random House, 1967. An analysis of the biker group from the New Journalist who spent time living with them.

Art and Literature

Baldwin, James. *The Fire Next Time*. New York: Dial Press, 1963. Essays on the tensions between blacks and whites.

Barth, John. *Giles Goat-Boy*. Garden City, NY: Doubleday & Co., 1987. A novel in which the university symbolizes the modern world.

Brautigan, Richard. *Trout Fishing in America, The Pill Versus the Spring Hill Mine Disaster*, and *In Watermelon Sugar*. Boston: Houghton Mifflin Company, 1989. A new collection of the poet's best-known works.

Chapman, Abraham, ed. *Black Voices: An Anthology of Afro-American Literature*. New York: New American Library, 1968. Works by Langston Hughes, Ralph Ellison, James Baldwin, Gwendolyn Brooks, and others.

Cleaver, Eldridge. *Soul on Ice*. New York: Dell Publishing Co., 1968. The author's observations on sexual and racial identity in the United States.

Clurman, Harold, ed. *Seven Plays of the Modern Theater*. New York: Grove Press, 1962. Includes *The Connection* and *The Balcony*, among others.

Didion, Joan. *Slouching towards Bethlehem.* New York: Farrar, Straus & Giroux, 1968. A collection of essays on California and the counterculture.

Fariña, Richard. *Been Down So Long It Looks Like Up to Me.* New York: Dell Publishing Co., 1966. The adventures of Gnossos Pappadapoulis.

Giovanni, Nikki. *Black Feeling Black Talk/Black Judgment.* New York: William Morrow, 1970. Poems on the black experience.

Kesey, Ken. *One Flew Over the Cuckoo's Nest.* New York: Viking Press, 1962. A novel that treats the brutality of a mental institution.

Mailer, Norman. *Armies of the Night.* New York: New American Library, 1968. A New-Journalistic treatment of the March on the Pentagon.

Robinson, William H. *NOMMO: An Anthology of Modern Black African and Black American Literature.* New York: Macmillan, 1972. Literature includes essays by H. Rap Brown and Eldridge Cleaver, fiction by Ishmael Reed, poetry by Sonia Sanchez, drama by Ed Bullins, and more.

Scheer, Robert, ed. *The Diary of Che Guevera.* New York: Bantam Books, 1968. The original version of the revolutionary's diary from November 7, 1966, to October 7, 1967, with Spanish text and photographs.

Wolfe, Tom. *The Electric Kool-Aid Acid Test.* New York: Farrar, Straus & Giroux, 1968. An account of the adventures of Ken Kesey and his Merry Pranksters.

X, Malcolm. *The Autobiography of Malcolm X.* New York: Ballantine Books, 1977. The life of the black revolutionary.

General Books

Albert, Judith, and Albert, Stewart. *The Sixties Papers.* New York: Praeger Press, 1984. Original documents from the Port Huron Statement to "The Myth of the Vaginal Orgasm."

McLuhan, Marshall. *The Medium Is the Message.* New York: Bantam Books, 1967. McLuhan's interpretation of the power of the media, in psychedelic prose.

Toffler, Alvin. *Future Shock.* New York: Random House, 1970. An analysis of social and other changes that Americans can expect.

BOOKS ABOUT THE ERA

Politics

Eisler, Anthony. *Bombs, Beards, and Barricades.* New York: Stein and Day, 1971. Traces 150 years of youth in revolt.

Fraser, Ronald, ed. *1968: A Student Generation in Revolt.* New York: Pantheon Books, 1988. Analyzes the year 1968 from Berkeley to Great Britain to Italy.

Goldman, Eric. *The Tragedy of Lyndon Johnson.* New York: Alfred A. Knopf, 1969. A biography of President Johnson.

Heath, Jim. *Decade of Disillusionment.* Bloomington, IN: University of Indiana Press, 1975. An analysis of the Kennedy and Johnson presidencies.

Hersh, Seymour M. *The Price of Power.* New York: Simon & Schuster, 1983. Kissinger's years in the White House.

Kaiser, Charles. *1968 in America.* New York: Weidenfield & Nicholson, 1988. A look at 1968 by a writer who was with the McCarthy campaign.

Miller, James. *Democracy Is in the Streets.* New York: Simon & Schuster, 1987. A discussion of the political counterculture, especially SDS, from Port Huron to the Siege of Chicago.

Vietnam

Baritz, Loren. *Backfire.* New York: Ballantine Books, 1988. An analysis of how our defeat in Vietnam was rooted in our culture.

Boettcher, Thomas. *Vietnam: The Valor and the Sorrow.* Boston: Little, Brown & Co., 1985. An in-depth study of the war in Vietnam.

Bowman, John F., ed. *The Vietnam War: An Almanac.* New York: Bison Books, 1985. A day-by-day guide to the Vietnam era.

Caputo, Philip. *A Rumor of War.* New York: Henry Holt & Co., 1977. The effects of the Vietnam War on those who fought it by a Marine who was one of the first into combat.

Dougan, Clark, et al. *A Nation Divided: The War at Home, 1945–1972.* Boston: Boston Publishing Co., 1984. What went on back in the States as the war was being waged in Southeast Asia.

Goldman, Peter, and Fuller, Tony. *Charlie Company.* New York: William Morrow, 1983. Surviving members of Charlie Company analyze their experiences in Vietnam.

Herr, Michael. *Dispatches.* New York: Avon Books, 1984. A freelance journalist's account of the Vietnam War from the perspective of the army "grunts" who fought it.

Newcomb, Richard. *A Pictorial History of the Vietnam War.* Garden City, NJ: Doubleday & Co., 1987. Pictures and text describe what happened in Vietnam.

Sheehan, Neil. *A Bright Shining Lie.* New York: Random House, 1988. A history of our involvement in Vietnam via a biography of Lieutenant Colonel John Paul Vann.

Civil Rights and Liberation

Branch, Taylor. *Parting the Waters: America in the King Years.* New York: Simon & Schuster, 1988. Volume one of a two-part history covering the civil rights movement from 1954 to 1963.

Cagin, Seth, and Dray, Philip. *We Are Not Afraid.* New York: Macmillan, 1988. The suspenseful story of what happened to civil rights workers Goodman, Schwerner, and Chaney in Mississippi.

Cohen, Marcia. *The Sisterhood: The True Story of the Women Who Changed the World.* New York: Simon & Schuster, 1988. Discussion of key figures in the feminist movement.

Geschwender, James A., ed. *The Black Revolt.* Englewood Cliffs, NJ: Prentice-Hall, 1971. Discusses the civil rights movement and ghetto uprisings.

Hole, Judith, and Levine, Ellen. *The Rebirth of Feminism.* New York: Quadrangle Books, 1971. A history of the feminist movement.

Williams, Juan. *Eyes on the Prize: America's Civil Rights Years.* New York: Penguin Books, 1987. A companion volume to the PBS series on the civil rights movement, covering the years 1954–1965.

The Counterculture

Berger, Bennett. *The Survival of a Counterculture.* Berkeley: University of California Press, 1981. A look at how the countercultural values and mores have survived to the present.

Jones, Mablen. *Getting It On: The Clothing of Rock 'n' Roll.* New York: Abbeville Press, 1987. What people wore from the golden age of rock through art rock.

Melinkoff, Ellen. *What We Wore.* New York: Quill Books, 1984. A history of clothing from 1950 to 1980.

Perry, Charles. *The Haight-Ashbury.* New York: Random House, 1984. A history of the Haight, from the first Acid Tests to the waning of the hippie movement.

Roszak, Theodore. *The Making of a Counterculture.* New York: Doubleday & Co., 1969. An analysis of what caused the rise of the counterculture and what it represented.

Stevens, Jay. *Storming Heaven: LSD and the American Dream.* New York: Harper & Row, 1987. The complete history of LSD, including the roles of Huxley, Sandoz Pharmaceuticals, and Leary, and its effects on the counterculture.

Sukenick, Ronald. *Down and In: Life in the Underground.* New York: Collier Books, 1987. Short-story and novel writer Sukenick tells about life in Greenwich Village from the fifties through the eighties.

Art and Literature

Anson, Robert Sam. *Gone Crazy and Back Again.* Garden City, NY: Doubleday & Co., 1981. A discussion of the founding of *Rolling Stone* and its role during the sixties.

Brustein, Robert. *The Theater of Revolt: An Approach to the Modern Drama.* Boston: Little, Brown & Co., 1964. An in-depth look at eight playwrights.

Downie, Leonard, Jr. *The New Muckrakers.* Washington, DC: The New Republic Book Co., 1976. Talks about New Journalism and underground newspapers and magazines.

Gilman, Richard. *The Confusion of Realms.* New York: Random House, 1969. Critical essays on Mailer, Barthelme, Sontag, and others.

Hassan, Ihab. *Contemporary American Literature, 1945–1972.* New York: Frederick Ungar Publishing Co., 1973. Analyzes poetry, fiction, and drama.

Herman, William. *Understanding Contemporary Drama.* Columbia, SC: University of South Carolina Press, 1987. A discussion of modern drama, including off- and off-off-Broadway.

Home, Steward. *The Assault on Culture.* London: Aporia Press & Unpopular Books, 1988. An analysis of various European and American art movements from the fifties through the eighties.

Kiernan, Robert F. *American Writing Since 1945: A Critical Survey.* New York: Frederick Ungar Publishing Co., 1983. From the beats to the New York poets to off-off-Broadway and more.

Peck, Abe. *Uncovering the Sixties: The Life and Times of the Underground Press.* New York: Pantheon Books, 1985. Identifies and gives the history of dozens of underground papers and magazines.

Whitmer, Peter, et al. *Aquarius Revisited: Seven Who Created the Sixties Counterculture that Changed America.* New York: Macmillan, 1987. Includes letters and interviews with Burroughs, Ginsberg, Kesey, Leary, Mailer, Tom Robbins, and Hunter S. Thompson.

Music

Duncan, Robert. *Only the Good Die Young.* New York: Harmony Books, 1986. Short biographies of music stars who died young, from Hank Williams to John Lennon.

Hendler, Herb. *Year by Year in the Rock Era.* New York: Praeger Press, 1987. Facts and trivia on all aspects of society during the rock years.

Nite, Norm. *Rock On.* Vol. 2. New York: Harper & Row, 1984. Information on bands and singers of the late sixties.

Pareles, Jon, and Romanowski, Patricia, eds. *The Rolling Stone Encyclopedia of Rock & Roll.* New York: Rolling Stone Press, 1983. Descriptions of singers and bands, trends in rock music, and hits of the rock era.

Taylor, Derek. *It Was Twenty Years Ago Today.* New York: Simon & Schuster, 1987. Focusing on the Beatles, this work is a collection of interviews of and about rock figures.

Ward, Ed, ed. *Rock of Ages: The Rolling Stone History of Rock 'n' Roll.* New York: Rolling Stone Press, 1986. A detailed history of rock and roll from its roots to the present.

General Books

Caute, David. *The Year of the Barricades: A Journey Through 1968.* New York: Harper & Row, 1988. From the Tet offensive to the civil rights movement to Kent State, this book traces the forces that led to the explosive year of 1968 and the events that resulted from it.

Gitlin, Todd. *The Sixties: Years of Hope, Days of Rage.* New York: Bantam Books, 1987. An account of the decade by an author and sociology professor who was an important member of the counterculture.

Gottlieb, Annie. *Do You Believe in Magic? The Second Coming of the Sixties Generation.* New York: Times Books, 1987. Interviews and recollections of the sixties by members of the counterculture.

Javna, John, and Javna, Gordon. *60s!* New York: St. Martin's Press, 1988. A compendium of facts and trivia about the decade.

Konig, Hans. *1968.* New York: W. W. Norton, 1987. A personal account of the events leading up to and occurring in the year 1968.

Matsutow, Allen J. *The Unraveling of America.* New York: Harper & Row, 1984. A scholarly history of liberalism during the sixties.

Morrison, Joan, and Morrison, Robert K. *From Camelot to Kent State: The Sixties Experience in the Words of Those Who Lived It.* New York: New York Times Books, 1987. Eighties interviews with people who were active in sixties organizations, from the Peace Corps to the Weathermen.

Viorst, Milton. *Fire in the Streets.* New York: Simon & Schuster, 1979. A detailed account of the counterculture in the sixties.

Weiner, Rex, and Stillman, Deanne. *Woodstock Census.* New York: Viking Press 1979. A survey of the sixties generation—what they are doing now and how they feel about their past.